DATE DUE

DEMCO, INC. 38-2931

Learnability in Optimality Theory

Learnability in Optimality Theory

Bruce Tesar and Paul Smolensky

The MIT Press
Cambridge, Massachusetts
London, England

This book was set in Times Roman by Best-set Typesetter Ltd., Hong Kong, in QuarkXPress and was printed and bound in the United States of America.

Library of Congress Cataloging-in-Publication Data

Tesar, Bruce
  Learnability in optimality theory/Bruce Tesar, Paul Smolensky.
      p.   cm.
  Includes bibliographical references and index.
  ISBN 0-262-20126-7
      1. Optimality theory (Linguistics)   2. Language acquisition.   3. Learning ability.
  I. Smolensky, Paul, 1955–   II. Title.
  P158.42.T47   2000
  401′.93—dc21   4/14/00   99-056826

Contents

Acknowledgments

This book emerged out of joint research conducted between 1993 and 1997. This work is significantly improved as a result of interactions with a great number of people. We have especially benefited from input provided by Jane Grimshaw, Bruce Hayes, John McCarthy, and, above all, Alan Prince. Among the numerous other people who have provided useful interactions are Eric Baković, Stefano Bertolo, Michael Brent, Luigi Burzio, Elan Dresher, Bob Frank, Peter Jusczyk, Ed Keer, Géraldine Legendre, Claartje Levelt, Clayton Lewis, Mark Liberman, Jim Martin, Mike Mozer, Joe Pater, Vieri Samek-Lodovici, Antonella Sorace, Suzanne Stevenson, Karin Stromswold, William Turkel, and Ken Wexler.

Multiple zip codes were inhabited by each of the authors during the development of this work. We would like to thank the Computer Science Department and the Institute for Cognitive Science of the University of Colorado at Boulder, the Cognitive Science Department of The Johns Hopkins University, and the Linguistics Department and the Center for Cognitive Science at Rutgers University, for institutional support. Bruce Tesar acknowledges the support of an NSF Graduate Fellowship, Paul Smolensky the support of a Guggenheim Fellowship and NSF Grants IIS-9720412 and IRI-9596120, and both authors the support of NSF Grants IRI-9213894 and BS-9209265.

We would also like to thank Amy Brand at The MIT Press for suggesting that a monograph was the way to go, and for expediting the publication process.

Finally, we would like to thank our families for all of their love and support: Esther Tesar, Géraldine Legendre, and Joshua Legendre Smolensky.

1 Language Learning

1.1 What This Book Is About

This book argues that the linguistic framework of *Optimality Theory* (OT) (Prince and Smolensky 1993) makes possible a particularly strong union of the interests of language learnability and linguistic theory. In support of this claim, a particular approach to language learning, *Robust Interpretive Parsing / Constraint Demotion* (RIP/CD), is presented and evaluated. This learning proposal is tightly bound to the central principles of OT, and the success of the learning proposal is evidence in favor of the main claim.

The language learning issue of primary concern in this book is the ambiguity of the overt information that constitutes the actual data received by a learner, and the resulting interdependence of the core grammar and the structural analysis of overt linguistic forms: which grammar a learner chooses depends on how they interpret the forms they hear, and which analysis they choose for a form depends on what grammar they are using. The RIP/CD proposal claims that this interdependence can be finessed by successive iteration: the learner can use a first guess at a grammar to estimate the structural analysis of the data, use the estimated analyses to improve the grammar, use the improved grammar to improve the analyses, and so forth. The learning procedure learns both the correct interpretations of the data and the correct grammar simultaneously. The viability of this "back-and-forth" strategy is heavily dependent on the use of OT to characterize the knowledge of language that the learner comes to possess.

The RIP/CD learning proposal is evaluated by a series of computer experiments, applying the proposal to overt data from a number of languages generated by an OT system for metrical stress. This system exhibits a nontrivial degree of ambiguity in the overt forms: most overt forms have several viable structural interpretations, with different interpretations favored by different grammars of the system. The performance is evaluated both on accuracy—whether or not the correct grammar was in fact learned—and computational efficiency—the amount of effort exerted during the process of learning the correct grammar.

The empirical results just mentioned are supported by stronger formal results concerning major parts of the proposal. It is not necessary to conduct any simulations to attempt to measure the amount of information required by the learner to determine the correct grammar, because of a strong upper bound on the amount of data required. This result, which applies to all language systems defined within OT, is proved correct in chapter 7. This result is an important part of the proposal made here, for it demonstrates that the adoption of OT guarantees a strong solution to one of the major issues in language learning.

Chapter 1 is devoted to laying out the larger context of this work, including the nature of relationships between learnability and universal grammar, and the background work on general learning theory that has informed and inspired the specific language learning proposal made here. Readers who would prefer to skip the background on the first reading are advised to jump to section 1.4, which presents a top-level outline of the proposals made in this book, along with pointers to the location of each topic within the book.

1.2 Learnability and Universal Grammar

It has become commonplace in generative linguistics circles to see the logical problem of language acquisition as a driving force in shaping grammatical theory (Chomsky 1981). The basic logic is essentially as follows. Learning a grammar is difficult because there are so many conceivable grammars and the available data is so impoverished. Thus a crucial job of a theory of universal grammar is to *restrict* the space of possible grammars the learner must consider, so that impoverished data may suffice to determine a correct grammar. This notion of restrictiveness is often reduced to the criterion that a satisfactory grammatical theory will delimit a finite set of possible grammars—distinguished from one another by the values of a finite number of *parameters*, for example. The fewer the possible grammars, the more learnable the theory.

Or so it would seem. In fact, however, limiting the set of possible grammars to a finite number serves only to improve the worst-case performance of the *least informed* learning method of all: exhaustive search, in which every possible hypothesis is examined. For, with finitely many possible grammars, search for a correct one is guaranteed to terminate eventually: at worst, once all possible grammars have been examined. With infinitely many possible grammars, such search may continue forever.

But comfort from the finiteness of the space of possible grammars is tenuous indeed. For a grammatical theory with an infinite number of possible grammars might be well structured, permitting *informed* search that converges quickly to the correct grammar—even though uninformed, exhaustive search is infeasible. And it is of little value that exhaustive search is guaranteed to terminate eventually when the space of possible grammars is finite, if the number of grammars is astronomical. In fact, a well-structured theory admitting an infinity of grammars could well be feasibly learnable,[1] while a poorly structured theory admitting a finite, but very large, number of possible grammars might not.

And indeed, a *principles-and-parameters* (P&P) *universal grammar* (UG) with n parameters admits at least 2^n grammars; more, if the parameters are not binary. Such exponential growth in the number of parameters quickly leads to spaces much too large to search exhaustively. An OT UG with N constraints admits $N!$ grammars, which grows still faster.

Thus to achieve meaningful assurance of learnability from our grammatical theory, we must seek evidence that the theory provides the space of possible grammars with the *kind of structure* that learning can effectively exploit.

Consider P&P theory in this regard. Two types of learnability research are useful as contrasts to the results we offer in this book. The first is *cue learning*, exemplified by work such as Dresher and Kaye 1990. These authors adopt a particular parameterized space of grammars, and analyze in great detail the relationships between the parameter settings and the forms overtly available to the learner. They propose a *specific* learning algorithm to make use of the structure provided by a *specific* P&P theory. Their analysis is entirely limited to their particular parametric system for metrical stress; a cue learning approach to a parametric grammar for some other component of linguistic theory, or even to an alternative parametric analysis of metrical stress, would essentially require starting over from scratch.

Another approach to learnability within P&P, quite different from cue learning, is represented in the work of Gibson and Wexler (1994) and Niyogi and Berwick (1996). The *triggering learning algorithm* (and its variations) is designed to learn grammars from data overtly available to the learner. Like those developed in our work, these algorithms apply to any instance of a very general class of systems: in their case, the class of P&P systems. Further, Niyogi and Berwick (1996) provide formal analysis of the algorithms. However, this work differs from ours in a direction representing the opposite extreme from cue learning: these learning algorithms are *minimally informed* by the grammatical theory. For triggering learning algorithms treat the grammar only as a black box evaluating learning data as either grammatically analyzable or not; the algorithms either randomly flip grammar parameters in order to render an input analyzable (Gibson and Wexler's *Triggering Learning Algorithm*), or randomly flip parameters without regard to immediate resulting analyzability (which, Niyogi and Berwick argue, can actually outperform the Triggering Learning Algorithm). These learning algorithms are equally appropriate as procedures for learning parameterized grammars and as procedures for, say, training a neural network[2] (with binary weights) to classify radar images of submarines: if flipping a parameter (connection in the network) gives better classification of a submarine, flip it. These are simply generic search algorithms that employ no properties of the grammatical theory per se.

Further, the learnability results relating to triggering learning algorithms assume the existence of overt data that directly reveal individual parameter values. Such an assumption limits how impoverished the learning data can be and has unclear relevance to realistic grammars (see Frank and Kapur 1996); we discuss this further in section 6.1. Finally, regardless of the availability of such "triggering" forms, these algorithms offer little justification for confidence in their tractability. In fact, the only result regarding the time required for learning is that the probability of learning the correct grammar increases toward 1 as the number of learning instances approaches infinity[3]—leaving open the possibility of doing even worse than exhaustive search.

In sum, these two approaches to learnability analysis within P&P either (1) use grammatical structure in the learning algorithm, but the structure of a *particular* parametric system, or (2) develop general algorithms applicable to any P&P system, but algorithms *so* general they apply just as well to any nongrammatical parameterized system. This dichotomy of approaches is likely a consequence of the nature of P&P. A particular P&P system, like one for stress, has sufficient structure to inform a learning procedure (option 1). But as a general theory of how grammars may differ (as opposed to how stress systems may differ), P&P provides little structure for a learner to exploit beyond the existence of a finite space for searching. In particular, P&P theory per se provides no characteristically *grammatical* structure for a language learner to exploit.

But the situation in OT is quite different. This theory is reviewed in chapter 2, but the immediately relevant claims of OT are these:

(1.1)   OT in a nutshell

· What is it that all languages have in common? *A set of constraints on well-formedness.*
· How may languages differ? *Only in which constraints have priority in case of conflict.*
· Language-particular relative constraint priorities are characterized by a *ranking* of the universal well-formedness constraints into a *dominance hierarchy*, with each constraint having absolute priority over all lower-ranked constraints.
· The grammar of a particular language—its constraint hierarchy—is an evaluator of structural descriptions, assigning a (nonnumerical) *Harmony* value that assesses the degree to which the constraints are met, taking into account the language-particular priorities. This provides the *harmonic ordering of forms*, ordering structural descriptions from maximal to minimal Harmony.
· The grammatical forms of the language are the *optimal* ones: the well-formed structural description of an input is the one with maximal Harmony.

Note that the constraints mentioned in (1.1) are the same in all languages: they contain no parameters. Unlike P&P, this is a theory of crosslinguistic variation with sufficient structure to enable grammatically informed learning algorithms independent of substantive grammatical assumptions.

(1.2)   Main claim of this book: OT is a theory of UG that provides sufficient structure at the level of the grammatical framework itself to allow general but grammatically informed learning algorithms to be formally defined. Further, the efficiency of the algorithms can be argued to follow in large part from the formal structure of the grammatical framework.

The algorithms we develop are procedures for learning the priority ranking of constraints that, by (1.1), is all that distinguishes the grammar of a particular language. These are unquestionably grammar learning algorithms, not generic search algorithms.[4] Yet the structure that makes these algorithms possible is not the structure of a theory of stress, nor a theory of phonology: it is the structure defining any OT grammar, that given in (1.1).

Of course, if a grammatically *un*informed learning algorithm, such as the Triggering Learning Algorithm, is desired, it can be obtained as easily in OT as in P&P; in fact, Pulleyblank and Turkel (1995, 1998) have already formulated and studied the *Constraint-Ranking Triggering Learning Algorithm*. Indeed, we can apply any of a number of generic search algorithms to the space of OT grammars—for example, Pulleyblank and Turkel (1995, 1998) have also applied the genetic algorithm to learning OT grammars. But unlike P&P, with OT we have an alternative to grammatically uninformed learning: learning algorithms specially constructed to exploit the structure provided by OT's theory of crosslinguistic variation.

1.3 Decomposing the Learning Problem

1.3.1 Grammar Learning and Robust Interpretive Parsing

To begin our analysis of grammar learning, we must distinguish the following three types of linguistic structure:

(1.3) The players in order of their appearance
- *Overt part of grammatical forms*: directly accessible to the learner
- *Full structural descriptions*: combine overt and nonovert ("hidden") structure
- *The grammar*: determines which structural descriptions are well formed

These three elements are all intimately connected, yet we propose to distinguish two subproblems, as schematically shown in figure 1.1.

(1.4) Decomposition of the problem
- *Robust interpretive parsing*: mapping the overt part of a form into a full structural description, complete with all hidden structure—given a grammar
- *Learning the grammar*—given a (robust) parser

(An interpretive parser is "robust" if it can parse an overt structure with a grammar, even when that structure is not grammatical according to the grammar. The importance of robustness will be discussed shortly.)

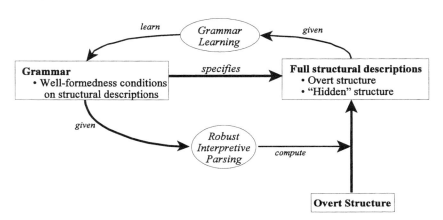

Figure 1.1
Problem decomposition

A competence theory of grammatical structure is most useful to an ultimate performance theory of language processing and acquisition when it provides sufficient structure so that procedures for both parsing and grammar learning can strongly exploit grammatical principles. Showing that this is indeed the case for OT is a major goal of our work.

We propose that the problems of parsing and grammar learning be decoupled to some degree. Such separation does at first seem problematic, however. One of the central difficulties of language learning, of course, is that grammars refer crucially to nonovert, hidden structure. Let us take the acquisition of stress as an expository example. The problem, then, is that the grammatical principles concern (say) metrical feet, yet these are hidden in the data presented to the learner: only the location of some stressed syllables is provided overtly. The learner cannot learn the metrical grammar until she knows where the feet lie, but she cannot know where the feet lie until she knows the grammar. We argue in section 1.3.2 that, despite this conundrum, partial decoupling of the parsing and learning problems is possible, and further, that such decoupling can enable powerful learning algorithms.

1.3.2   Iterative Model–Based Solutions to the Problem of Learning Hidden Structure

The learner cannot deduce the hidden structure in learning data until she has learned the grammar, but she cannot learn the grammar until she has the hidden structure. This feature of the language learning problem is challenging indeed—but not at all special to language, as it turns out. Even in such mundane contexts as a computer learning to recognize handwritten digits, the same problem arises. Given an example of a 5, the computer needs to adapt its model for what makes a good 5. But in many cases, the system is not told which digit a given training example exemplifies: it is often impractical for all the digits in a huge training corpus to be hand labeled as to what category they belong to, so the computer is forced to learn which digits *are* 5s at the same time as learning what makes a *good* 5. The computer-learner cannot improve its model of what makes a well-formed 5 until it knows when it is seeing a 5, but it cannot know when it has seen a 5 until it knows what makes a well-formed 5.

This problem has been extensively studied in the learning theory literature (often under the label *unsupervised learning*; e.g., Hinton 1989). Much of the work has addressed automatic speech recognition, mostly under the name *Hidden Markov Models* (Baum and Petrie 1966; Bahl, Jelinek, and Mercer 1983; Brown et al. 1990). These speech systems are simultaneously learning (1) when the acoustic data they are "hearing" is an example of, say, a (hidden) phone [f], and (2) what makes for a good [f].

This problem has been successfully addressed, in theory and practice. The necessary formalization is approximately as follows. A parameterized system (e.g., a neural network) is assumed that, given the values of hidden variables, produces the probabilities that overt variables will have various values: this is the *model* of the relation between hidden and overt variables. (As we will see shortly, this model corresponds to the grammar in our problem.) Given a hidden [f] in a sequence of phones, such a model would specify the probabilities of different acoustic values in the portion of the acoustic stream corresponding to the hidden [f]. The learning system needs to learn the correct model parameters so that hidden [f]s will be associated with the correct acoustic values, at the same time it is learning to classify all acoustic tokens of [f]s as being of type [f]. The general problem is usually formalized along the lines indicated in (1.5).

(1.5)   Problem of Learning Hidden Structure

Given: A set of overt learning data (e.g., acoustic data) and a parameterized model that relates overt information to hidden structure (e.g., phones)

Find: A set of model parameters such that the hidden structure assigned to the data by the model makes the overt data most probable (this model "best explains" the data)

There is a class of successful algorithms for solving this problem, the most important of which is the *Expectation Maximization* (EM) algorithm (Dempster, Laird, and Rubin 1977; for recent tutorial introductions, see Nádas and Mercer 1996, Smolensky 1996c). The basic idea common to this class of algorithms, which we will call *iterative model–based learning algorithms*, is characterized in highly general terms in (1.6).

(1.6) Iterative model–based solution to the Problem of Learning Hidden Structure

Adopt some initial model of the relation between hidden and overt structure; this can be a random set of parameter values, or a more informed initial guess.

Step 1: Given this initial model, and given some overt learning data, find the hidden structure that makes the observed data most probable according to the model.[5] Hypothesizing this hidden structure provides the best explanation of the overt data, assuming the current (initially poor) model. This first step of the algorithm is performed on all the available data.

Step 2: Now that we have deduced some hidden structure (initially incorrect), we use it to improve our model, in the second step of the algorithm. Since all the overt (acoustic) data have been connected to corresponding hidden (phonemic) structure, we can now improve the model, changing its parameters so that the imputed hidden structure optimally predicts the actual overt structure observed. (For example, the model for hidden phone [f] is changed so that it now predicts as closely as possible the actual acoustic values in the data that have been identified as instances of [f].)

Now that the model has been changed, it will assign different (generally more correct) hidden structure to the original overt data. So the algorithm goes back through the data and executes step 1 over again, reassigning hidden structure.

This new assignment of hidden structure permits step 2 to be repeated, leading to a new (generally improved) model. And so the algorithm executes steps 1 and 2 repeatedly.

This is summarized in row (a) of table 1.1.[6]

In various formalizations, iterative model–based algorithms have been shown to converge to a model that is in some sense optimal. In practice, convergence often occurs rather quickly, even with a relatively poor initial model. The key to constructing a successful iterative algorithm is combining correct solutions to the two subproblems addressed in steps 1 and 2. Crucially, *correct* here means finding the correct solution to one subproblem, assuming that the other subproblem has been correctly solved. This is summarized in (1.7).

(1.7)   Correctness criteria for solutions of iterative model–based subproblems

For step 1: Given the correct *model* of overt/hidden relations, correctly compute the hidden structure that is *most probable* when paired with the overt data.

For step 2: Given the correct hidden structure, correctly compute the *model* that makes the given pairing of overt and hidden structure *most probable*.

The iterative model–based approach to learning can be connected directly with OT with the mediation of a piece of neural network theory called *Harmony Theory* (Smolensky 1983, 1986). In Harmony Theory, the well-formedness of a representation in a neural network is numerically measured by its Harmony value, and the probability of a representation is governed by its Harmony: the greater the Harmony, the higher the

Table 1.1
Iterative model-based learning algorithms

Framework		Iterative Solution Steps	
		Step 1 **Find the hidden structure…**	**Step 2** **Find…**
(a)	Iterative Model	… that is most probable when paired with the overt data, given the current model.	… the model that makes step 1's pairing most probable.
(b)	Harmonic Grammar	… that is most harmonic (numeric) when paired with the overt data, given the current grammar.	… the grammar that makes step 1's pairing of overt and hidden structure most harmonic (numeric).
(c)	OT **RIP/CD**	… of the most harmonic (OT) structural description consistent with the overt data, given the current grammar. **Robust Interpretive Parsing**	… a grammar that makes step 1's structural description optimal. **Constraint Demotion**

probability.[7] A representation has a hidden part and an overt part, and the Harmony function provides the model that relates these two parts: given some overt structure, associating it with different hidden structures leads to different Harmony values (and hence different probabilities). In step 1 of the iterative learning algorithm (1.6), given some overt learning data we find the hidden structure that makes the overt data most probable. This means finding the hidden structure that maximizes Harmony, when associated with the given overt structure. In step 2, we use this hidden structure to change the model—that is, change the Harmony function so that the just-derived hidden/overt associations have the greatest possible Harmony.

In Harmonic Grammar (Legendre, Miyata, and Smolensky 1990a, 1990b), an application of Harmony Theory to linguistics, the overt and hidden structures are part of linguistic structural descriptions, and the model that governs the relation between overt and hidden structure is a grammar. In this context, the iterative model algorithm in table 1.1(a) becomes the Harmonic Grammar algorithm of table 1.1(b), and the correctness criteria are like those in (1.7), but with *grammar* in place of *model*, and *harmonic* in place of *probable*. In this case, *harmonic* refers to the numeric conception of Harmony used in Harmony Theory.

In OT, the Harmony of structural descriptions is computed from the grammar nonnumerically, and there is (as yet) no probabilistic interpretation of Harmony. But the learning procedure of table 1.1(b) is still perfectly well defined; it is summarized in table 1.1(c) and labeled RIP/CD, for *Robust Interpretive Parsing / Constraint Demotion*. Robust interpretive parsing (further discussed in section 1.3.3) is the procedure that will be used to perform the hidden structure assignment of step 1. Constraint Demotion (presented in chapter 3) is the procedure that will be used to perform the grammar learning of step 2.

Given some overt learning data, RIP/CD first computes the hidden structure that has maximal Harmony when combined with the overt structure. Given learning data consisting of a sequence of syllables with stresses, for example, we find the foot structure that, in combination with the given stress pattern, has maximal Harmony. Which foot structure this is depends jointly on the overt stresses and on the currently assumed grammar—the current ranking of metrical constraints. So the algorithm proceeds as follows. Start with an initial grammar (the selection of an initial grammar is further discussed in chapter 5). In step 1 (the RIP step), use this grammar to assign (initially incorrect) hidden structure to the overt learning data by maximizing Harmony. In step 2 (the CD step), use this hidden structure to learn a new grammar, one in which each combined hidden/overt structure of the currently analyzed data has higher Harmony than all its competitors. With this improved grammar, return to step 1 and repeat.

The prospects of success for this algorithm are supported by the fact that the analogous "correctness" criteria are met. When translated from the probabilistic framework into the OT framework, the correctness criteria given in (1.7) become those stated in (1.8).

(1.8)   Correctness criteria for solutions to the subproblems under OT

For step 1, robust interpretive parsing: Given the correct *grammar* of overt/hidden relations, correctly compute the hidden structure that is *most harmonic* when paired with the overt data.
For step 2, grammar learning: Given the correct hidden structure, correctly compute the *grammar* that makes the given pairing of overt and hidden structure *optimal*.

Procedures for performing robust interpretive parsing are discussed in section 1.3.3 (general parsing with OT grammars is discussed at greater length in chapter 8). The Constraint Demotion algorithm for grammar learning is presented and discussed at length in chapter 3. The correctness of the Constraint Demotion algorithm (i.e., that it satisfies the second criterion specified in 1.8) is a theorem; the full proofs are given in chapter 7. The performance of the overall RIP/CD algorithm is explored in chapter 4, where results are presented for simulations applying this algorithm to the learning of metrical stress. The results presented in this book are from the latest and most extensive simulations of this algorithm. For the results of earlier studies, see Tesar 1997, 1998b.

1.3.3   Remarks on Parsing

Step 1 of our problem decomposition, given in table 1.1(c), makes it essential that we have a parser that can use a grammar to assign hidden structure to overt forms that are not grammatical according to that very grammar: this is what we mean by *robustness*. Our problem decomposition, we can now see, imposes a seemingly paradoxical requirement. An overt form will be informative (allow the learner to improve the grammar) if the current grammar (incorrectly) declares it to be ungrammatical. Step 1 of the RIP/CD algorithm requires that we use our current (incorrect) grammar to parse this input (assign it hidden structure), even though the grammar declares it ill formed. For many formal grammars, such an ungrammatical form is, by definition, unparsable, yet step 1 requires the grammar to parse it just the same.

OT grammars can easily cope with this demand. An OT grammar provides a harmonic ordering of all full structural descriptions, as described in (1.1). This harmonic ordering can be used in a variety of ways. The customary use is as follows: Given an input I, $Gen(I)$ is the set of all structural descriptions of I; we find the maximal-Harmony member of this set, and it is the output assigned to I. This use of the grammar corresponds to the "language generation" problem of computational linguistics, or the "language production" problem of psycholinguistics. We will call this *production-directed parsing* to contrast it with the interpretive parsing used in RIP/CD.

But, as proposed in Smolensky 1996a and developed in Tesar 1999, harmonic ordering can be used for the "language interpretation" or "language comprehension" problem as well. In this problem, we are given an overt "phonetic" form φ. The set $Int(\varphi)$ is the class of all structural descriptions with overt part equal to φ. Let us call the maximal-Harmony member of this set the *interpretive parse* assigned to φ by the grammar. Crucially for present purposes, this interpretation process makes sense even when the grammar declares φ ungrammatical (i.e., even when there is no input I for which the optimal member of $Gen(I)$ has overt form φ). An algorithm that can compute this mapping from φ to its interpretative parse is thus a robust interpretive parser capable of performing step 1 of the RIP/CD algorithm.

The most significant and general result, then, is the observation that the structure of OT grammars makes it possible to coherently define robust interpretive parsing. This definition works for any OT system. Further, the function computed by robust interpretive parsing, when given the correct grammar for a language, is the problem of "language comprehension" under OT. Thus, the assumption that robust interpretive parsing can be effectively computed is really little more than the assumption that language comprehension can be effectively computed, an assumption most work on language learnability uncontroversially relies on.

While it is not conceptually possible to provide parsing algorithms that will work for every conceivable OT system, parsing algorithms have been developed for particular linguistically interesting classes of OT systems. For production-directed parsing, algorithms of several kinds have been developed. The production-directed parsing algorithm used in the simulations of this book comes from a class of OT parsing algorithms based on dynamic programming (Tesar 1995, 1996). Under general formal assumptions on *Gen* and *Con*, these algorithms are proved correct and efficient. The algorithms used in this book's simulations have a time complexity that is linear in the length of the input—for example, for syllabification, the amount of computation required grows linearly with the number of segments in the input. Other production-directed parsing algorithms for various classes of OT systems have also been developed (Ellison 1994, Eisner 1997, Frank and Satta 1998, Karttunen 1998).

Robust interpretive parsing algorithms have also been developed for specific classes of OT systems. The robust interpretive parsing algorithm used in the simulations of this book (Tesar 1999) is quite similar to its production-directed parsing counterpart and shares the linear computational complexity. The algorithm is a member of a class of interpretive parsing algorithms that apply to cases where the underlying form is contained within the overt form, so that hidden structure consists entirely of structural (not lexical) information.

1.3.4 Remark on Grammar Learning from Full Structural Descriptions

Given the decomposition of the learning problem developed in this section, the subproblem of grammar learning is the problem of finding a correct grammar given learning data consisting of grammatical full structural descriptions. This is the central problem solved by the Constraint Demotion algorithms developed later.

On first glance, this problem may seem trivial, since knowing the full structural descriptions provides considerable information about the grammar that is not evident in the overt data. What this first glance fails to perceive is that in OT, the grammatical principles (constraints) interact in a rich, complex way. There is nothing like a transparent mapping from the hidden structure to the grammar: the explanatory power of OT lies precisely in the diversity of structural consequences of a constraint embedded within a hierarchy. Knowing the location of the metrical feet in a word, for example, leaves one far short of knowing the metrical grammar. An OT grammar is a collection of violable constraints, and any given foot structure will typically involve the violation of many different constraints: many language-particular OT grammars will be consistent with the given foot structure. Linguists who have actually faced the problem of deducing OT grammars from a complete set of full structural descriptions can attest to the nontriviality of solving this problem, especially in the general case. Indeed, the algorithms presented here (in chapter 3) have significant practical value for linguists working in OT. Given hypothesized structural descriptions of language data and a hypothesized set of constraints, these algorithms can quickly and easily provide a class of constraint rankings that account for the data, or directly determine that no such rankings exist.

1.4 Outline of the Book

The following is a guide to the main proposals of this book and where they may be found.

The central claim of the book, stated in (1.2), is that OT provides sufficient structure at the level of the grammatical framework itself to allow general but grammatically informed learning algorithms to be formally defined. Specifically, an algorithm is proposed in which the interdependence of grammars and structural descriptions is overcome by using successive approximation, iterating between "robust interpretive parsing" to assign structure to overt data, and grammar learning from the assigned structure. This proposal, named RIP/CD for robust interpretive parsing / Constraint Demotion, was introduced in section 1.3.

RIP/CD relies heavily on the structure of OT. An overview of OT, including illustrations with OT analyses of syllable structure and clausal subject distribution, is presented in chapter 2.

RIP/CD employs a decomposition of learning into two central subproblems. The first subproblem is that of assigning a structural description to an overt linguistic form given a grammar that may not be correct. This is the computation named robust interpretive parsing. Section 1.3.3 showed how this problem may be formally characterized within OT as optimization over a space of candidates all of which match the overt linguistic form. Concrete algorithms for computing robust interpretive parsing are discussed in section 8.5 of chapter 8, devoted to parsing algorithms for classes of OT grammars.

The second subproblem of RIP/CD is the learning of a constraint ranking from a set of full structural descriptions. This problem is solved by a family of algorithms based on the principle of Constraint Demotion. This principle states that constraints violated by grammatical structural descriptions must be demoted (in the ranking) below constraints violated by competing structural descriptions. Constraint Demotion is presented in chapter 3, where it is illustrated and discussed.

Constraint Demotion has two important formal properties. First, it is guaranteed to learn a correct ranking from an adequate data set. Second, there is a strict bound on the amount of data needed to form an adequate data set: Constraint Demotion will never need more than $N(N - 1)$ informative examples to correctly determine the grammar (where N is the number of constraints). Formal proofs of these results are given in chapter 7.

Constraint demotion reranks constraints based on the relative constraint violation patterns of structural descriptions of (1) grammatical forms, and (2) some competing forms. It thus depends on an ability to efficiently compute (1) structural descriptions of overt learning data, and (2) informative competing structural descriptions. Computation of the first is achieved by robust interpretive parsing, as discussed earlier. Computation of the second, informative competitors, is achieved by production-directed parsing, the very same computational procedure at work in language production. The use of production-directed parsing in learning is discussed in section 3.3; algorithms for performing production-directed parsing are presented in an chapter 8.

Given concrete proposals for solving the two subproblems, it is possible to evaluate RIP/CD, the strategy of iterating between structure assignment and ranking adjustment. Such an evaluation is conducted here through a series of experiments using a computer implementation of RIP/CD applied to an OT system for metrical stress. Many of the overt forms in the languages of this system have a nontrivial degree of ambiguity—the same overt form is consistent with several different possible structural descriptions—so this is a meaningful test. The experimental results are presented and discussed in chapter 4.

Given a credible approach to learning grammars by unraveling the basic interdependence between structural descriptions and constraint rankings, the possibility of multiple grammars consistent with the same data may be raised. In particular, the familiar issue of subset relations among different languages can be raised: Can the learner be constrained so as to always select the smallest language consistent with the positive data presented? This question is briefly discussed in section 5.1, along with a proposed solution: set the initial state of the learner to a ranking in which all markedness constraints dominate all faithfulness constraints.

One key component of the language learning problem that remains is the language-specific inventory of lexical underlying forms, which clearly must also be learned. The problem is made challenging by an interdependence quite similar to that addressed by RIP/CD: the actual form of the lexical entries is dependent on the constraint ranking, and vice versa. Section 5.2 discusses the prospects for extending the same iterative strategy embodied by RIP/CD to include the simultaneous learning of rankings and lexical underlying forms.

Chapter 6 revisits the larger issue of the relationship between learnability and linguistic theory, the issue first discussed in section 1.2. This chapter discusses the observation that the approach to language learning proposed in this book is not at all neutral with respect to linguistic theory: it is highly specific to OT. Further, this approach to learning actually thrives when substantive universal principles interact strongly in the determination of linguistic patterns, a property hardly universal among language learning proposals. The consequence is that the demands of linguistic explanation and the requirements of language learnability converge and are mutually supportive. We take this convergence as evidence that OT, and RIP/CD, are on the right track.

2 An Overview of Optimality Theory

This chapter presents the fundamental principles of OT. The defining reference is by Prince and Smolensky (1993) (abbreviated *P&S* here). Sections 2.1 and 2.2 provide the basics of the linguistic theory, while section 2.3 formulates the precise grammar learning problem posed by OT. Readers familiar with OT may wish to move directly to section 2.3.

We present the basics of OT as a series of general principles. To underscore the generality of the grammatical theory and our learnability analysis, we exemplify these principles with two running examples, one in phonology and one in syntax. The phonological example is the Basic CV Syllable Theory of P&S (chapter 6); we abbreviate this *CVT*. Our syntactic example is the theory of the distribution of clausal subjects proposed in Grimshaw and Samek-Lodovici 1995 (see also Samek-Lodovici 1994, 1996; Grimshaw and Samek-Lodovici 1998); we dub this theory *GSL*. Both examples will be used in chapter 3 to illustrate the Constraint Demotion learning procedure.

2.1 Constraints and Their Violation

Our starting point is a very basic principle.

(2.1)   Grammars specify functions.
A grammar specifies a function that assigns to each input a structural description or output. (A grammar per se does not provide an algorithm for computing this function, e.g., by sequential derivation.)

In CVT, an input is a string of C's and V's—for example, /VCVC/. An output is a parse of the string into syllables, denoted as in (2.2).

(2.2)   Examples of the input string /VCVC/ parsed into syllables
a. .V.CVC.   = [$_\sigma$ V] [$_\sigma$ CVC]
b. ⟨V⟩.CV.⟨C⟩ = V [$_\sigma$ CV] C
c. ⟨V⟩.CV.C□̣. = V [$_\sigma$ CV] [$_\sigma$ C□̣]
d. .□V.CV.⟨C⟩ = [$_\sigma$ □V] [$_\sigma$ CV] C

Output (2.2a) is an onsetless open syllable followed by a closed syllable (periods denote the boundaries of syllables). Output (2.2b) contains only one, open, syllable. The initial V and final C of the input are not parsed into syllable structure, as notated by the angle brackets ⟨⟩. These segments exemplify *underparsing* and are not phonetically realized, so

(2.2b) is "pronounced" simply as .CV. The form .CV. is the *overt form* contained in (2.2b). Output (2.2c) consists of a pair of open syllables, in which the nucleus of the second syllable is not filled by an input segment. This empty nucleus is notated ⊡ and exemplifies *overparsing*. The phonetic interpretation of this empty nucleus is an epenthetic vowel. Thus (2.2c) has .CV.CV. as its overt form. As in (2.2b), the initial V of the input is unparsed in (2.2c). Output (2.2d) is also a pair of open syllables (phonetically, .CV.CV.), but this time it is the onset of the first syllable that is unfilled (notated ☐; phonetically, an epenthetic consonant), while the final C is unparsed.

In Grimshaw and Samek-Lodovici's theory, GSL, an input is "a lexical head with a mapping of its argument structure into other lexical heads, plus a tense specification . . . as in Grimshaw (1997). The . . . input also specifies which arguments are foci, and which arguments are coreferent with the topic" (Grimshaw and Samek-Lodovici 1995:590). The example we will use is shown in (2.3); it represents the predicate *sing*, in the present perfect tense, with a masculine singular argument that is the current discourse topic.

An output in GSL is an X′ structure, a possible extended projection for the lexical head in the sense of Grimshaw 1990.

(2.3)   Some outputs for the input $I \equiv \langle$sing(x), x = topic, x = he;Tense = present perfect$\rangle$
a. [$_{IP}$ has [sung]]
b. [$_{IP}$ he$_i$ has [t$_i$ sung]]
c. [$_{IP}$ has [[t$_i$ sung] he$_i$]]
d. [$_{IP}$ it   has [[t$_i$ sung] he$_i$]]

In the following discussion, these outputs will consistently be labeled (a)–(d) as in (2.3). Output (a) is a clause with no subject: the highest projection of the verb, labeled IP, has no Spec position. Output (b) has *he* in SpecIP, co-indexed with a trace in SpecVP. Output (c) has no SpecIP position, and *he* right-adjoined to VP, co-indexed with a trace in SpecVP; output (d) is the same, but with an expletive subject in SpecIP.

The second principle of OT is a prerequisite for the competition involved in the determination of optimality.

(2.4)   *Gen*: UG provides a function *Gen* that, given any input *I*, generates *Gen*(*I*), the set of candidate structural descriptions for *I*.

The input I is an identified substructure contained within each of its candidate outputs in $Gen(I)$. The domain of Gen implicitly defines the space of possible inputs.

In CVT, for any input I, the candidate outputs in $Gen(I)$ consist of all possible parses of the string into syllables, including the possible over- and underparsing structures exemplified in (2.2b)–(2.2d). All syllables are assumed to contain a nucleus position, with optional preceding onset and following coda positions. CVT adopts the simplifying assumption (true of many languages) that the syllable position's onset and coda may each contain at most one C, and the nucleus position may contain at most one V. The four candidates of /VCVC/ in (2.2) are only illustrative of the full set $Gen(/VCVC/)$. Since the possibilities of overparsing are un-limited, $Gen(/VCVC/)$ in fact contains an infinite number of candidates.

For the syntactic input $I \equiv \langle sing(x), \ldots \rangle$ given in (2.3), $Gen(I)$ includes the four X′-structure outputs (2.3a)–(2.3d), along with others such as the entirely empty *null parse*, Ø. Each structural description of I in $Gen(I)$ should be understood to include I itself as a subpart, along with the output X′ structure. Following McCarthy and Prince 1995, we may assume that each structural description includes a *correspondence relation* linking the lexical heads in I with their correspondents in the output. Output (2.3a), [IP has [sung]], displays *underparsing*: an element of the input, x, has no correspondent in the output. Output (2.3d), [IP it has [[t$_i$ sung] he$_i$]], displays *overparsing*: an element of the output, *it*, has no cor-respondent in the input.

The next principle identifies the formal character of substantive gram-matical principles.

(2.5)   *Con*: UG provides a set *Con* of universal well-formedness constraints[1].

The constraints in *Con* evaluate the candidate outputs for a given input in parallel (i.e., simultaneously). Given a candidate output, each constraint assesses a multiset of *marks*, where each mark corresponds to one violation of the constraint. The collection of all marks assessed a can-didate parse p is denoted *marks*(p). A mark assessed by a constraint $\mathbb{C}$ is denoted *$\mathbb{C}$. A parse p_x is more marked than a parse p_y with respect to $\mathbb{C}$ if and only if $\mathbb{C}$ assesses more marks to p_x than to p_y. (The theory recognizes the notions more and less marked, but not absolute numeri-cal levels of markedness.)

The CVT constraints are given in (2.6).

(2.6) Basic CV Syllable Theory constraints[2]
a. ONSET: Syllables have onsets.
b. NOCODA: Syllables do *not* have codas.
c. PARSE: Underlying (input) material is parsed into syllable structure.
d. FILL^{Nuc}: Nucleus positions are filled with underlying material.
e. FILL^{Ons}: Onset positions (when present) are filled with underlying material.

These constraints can be illustrated with the candidate outputs in (2.2a)–(2.2d). The marks incurred by these candidates are summarized in table 2.1. This is an OT *constraint tableau*. The competing candidates are shown in the left column. The other columns are for the universal constraints, each indicated by the label at the top of the column. Constraint violations are indicated with asterisks, one for each violation.

Candidate (2.2a) = .V.CVC. violates ONSET in its first syllable and NOCODA in its second; the remaining constraints are satisfied. The single mark that ONSET assesses .V.CVC. is denoted *ONSET. This candidate is a *faithful* parse: it involves neither underparsing nor overparsing, and therefore satisfies the *faithfulness* constraints PARSE and FILL[3]. By contrast, (2.2b) = ⟨V⟩.CV.⟨C⟩ violates PARSE, and more than once. This tableau will be further explained later.

The GSL constraints are given in (2.7) (Grimshaw and Samek-Lodovici 1995:590).

(2.7) Constraints of the GSL theory of subjects
a. SUBJ(ECT): The highest A-specifier in an extended projection must be filled (Grimshaw 1997).

Table 2.1
Constraint tableau for L_1

Candidates	ONSET	NOCODA	FILL^{Nuc}	PARSE	FILL^{Ons}
/VCVC/ →					
☞ (d) .□V.CV.⟨C⟩				*	*
(b) ⟨V⟩.CV.⟨C⟩				* *	
(c) ⟨V⟩.CV.C□.			*	*	
(a) .V.CVC.	*	*			

b. FULL-INT(ERPRETATION): Elements of the output must be interpreted (Grimshaw 1997).

c. DROP-TOP(IC): Arguments coreferent with the topic are structurally unrealized.

d. AL(IGN)-FOC(US): The left edge of a focused constituent is aligned with the right edge of a maximal projection.

e. PARSE: Input constituents are parsed (have a correspondent in the output).

These constraints can be illustrated with the candidate outputs in (2.3), as shown in table 2.2. (In all candidates, ALIGN-FOCUS is vacuously satisfied, because this input has no focus.) We can interpret PARSE and FULL-INTERPRETATION as members of the FAITHFULNESS family of constraints, which play the important role in OT of requiring that an output faithfully parse its input: each input element has one output correspondent with identical featural content, and vice versa. (Relative to OT phonology, the technical details of FAITHFULNESS in OT syntax are more obviously an open question for research. In phonology the "vocabulary" of the input and output are more nearly identical, so requiring one-to-one correspondence between input and output is more straightforward.)

2.2 Optimality and Harmonic Ordering

In OT, each underlying form is assigned a structural description, selected from the set of possible candidates. The selected candidate is, by definition, the grammatical candidate. The basis for this selection is the constraint violations assessed to each candidate. Intuitively, the grammatical candidate should be the one "least offensive" to the constraints. However, constraints can conflict, and the case shown in table 2.1, with

Table 2.2
Constraint violations in GSL

$\langle$sing(x), x = topic, x = he; T = pres perf$\rangle$	PARSE	SUBJ	FULL-INT	DROP-TOP	AL-FOC
(b) [$_{IP}$ he$_I$ has [t$_i$ sung]]				*	
(d) [$_{IP}$ it has [[t$_i$ sung] he$_i$]]			*	*	
(c) [$_{IP}$ has [[t$_i$ sung] he$_i$]]		*		*	
(a) [$_{IP}$ has [sung]]	*	*			

every candidate violating at least one constraint, is by far the most common. Thus, the grammar needs a basis for resolving such conflicts.

OT gives a quite specific and restrictive theory of how constraint conflict is resolved. In a given language, different constraints are assigned different priority levels. When a choice must be made between satisfying one constraint or another, the stronger must take priority. The result is that the weaker will be violated in a grammatical structural description.

(2.8)　*Constraint ranking*: A grammar *ranks* the universal constraints in a *dominance hierarchy*.

When one constraint $\mathbb{C}_1$ dominates another constraint $\mathbb{C}_2$ in the hierarchy, the relation is denoted $\mathbb{C}_1 \gg \mathbb{C}_2$. The ranking defining a grammar is total; the hierarchy determines the relative dominance of every pair of constraints: $\mathbb{C}_1 \gg \mathbb{C}_2 \gg \ldots \gg \mathbb{C}_n$.

(2.9)　*Harmonic ordering (H-eval)*: A grammar's constraint ranking induces a harmonic ordering $\prec$ of all structural descriptions. Two candidate structural descriptions D_1 and D_2 are compared by identifying the highest-ranked constraint $\mathbb{C}_x$ with respect to which D_1 and D_2 are not equally marked. The candidate less marked with respect to $\mathbb{C}_x$ is the more harmonic, or the one with higher Harmony (with respect to the given ranking).

$D_1 \prec D_2$ denotes that D_1 is less harmonic than D_2. The harmonic ordering $\prec$ determines the relative Harmony of every pair of candidates. For a given input, the most harmonic of the candidate outputs provided by *Gen* is the optimal candidate: it is the one assigned to the input by the grammar. Only this optimal candidate is well formed (grammatical); all less harmonic candidates are ill formed.

Given the definition of grammaticality in terms of relative Harmony, along with the requirement that grammars be defined by total rankings of the constraints, there is only one possible way that more than one competing candidate can be simultaneously grammatical: both candidates must have identical constraint violations. Two candidates assessed exactly the same marks by all the constraints cannot be distinguished on the basis of *any* constraint ranking relation and will always be equally harmonic. If two (or more) candidates have equal Harmony, and both are more harmonic than all the other candidates, the two candidates are both optimal, with the interpretation of free alternation. If candidates D_1 and D_2 have equal Harmony, that relationship is denoted $D_1 \sim D_2$. In practice, it is quite rare to have more than one optimal candidate for any given input.

A couple of properties are worth stressing. First, the harmonic evaluation of candidates is purely relative, with no significance attached to the absolute number or distribution of constraint violations assessed to a candidate. A candidate with 150 constraint violations is no less grammatical for it, provided it better satisfies the ranked constraints than any of its competitors. Second, the only comparisons directly relevant to the grammaticality of forms are those between the optimal candidate and its competitors. The relative Harmony, with respect to each other, of two suboptimal candidates is assigned no significant interpretation. One suboptimal competitor is not "closer to grammatical" than another even though it is more harmonic than the other.

A formulation of harmonic ordering that will prove quite useful for learning involves *Mark Cancelation*. Consider a pair of competing candidates D_a and D_b, with corresponding lists of violation marks *marks(D_a)* and *marks(D_b)*. Mark Cancelation is a process applied to a pair of lists of marks: it cancels violation marks in common to the two lists. Thus, if a constraint C_x assesses one or more marks $*C_x$ in both *marks(D_a)* and *marks(D_b)*, an instance of $*C_x$ is removed from each list, and the process is repeated until at most one of the lists still contains a mark $*C_x$. (Note that if D_a and D_b are equally marked with respect to C_x, the two lists contain equally many marks $*C_x$, and all occurrences of $*C_x$ are eventually removed.) The resulting lists of *uncanceled marks* are denoted *marks'* (D_a) and *marks'(D_b)*. If a mark $*C_x$ remains in the uncanceled mark list of D_a, then D_a is more marked with respect to C_x. If the highest-ranked constraint assessing an uncanceled mark has a mark in *marks'(D_a)*, then $D_a < D_b$: this is the definition of harmonic ordering $<$ in terms of Mark Cancelation. Mark Cancelation is indicated by "crossing out the marks" in the tableau in table 2.3: one mark *Parse cancels between the candidates (d) and (b) of table 2.1, and one uncanceled mark *Parse remains in *marks'(b)*.

Defining grammaticality via harmonic ordering has an important consequence.

Table 2.3
Mark Cancelation

Candidates	ONSET	NOCODA	FILL^{Nuc}	PARSE	FILL^{Ons}
(d) .□V.CV.⟨C⟩				✗	*
(b) ⟨V⟩.CV.⟨C⟩				✗	*

(2.10)   *Minimal violation*: The grammatical candidate minimally violates the constraints, relative to the constraint ranking.

The constraints of UG are *violable*: they are potentially violated in well-formed structures. Such violation is *minimal*, however, in the sense that the grammatical candidate D for an input I will best satisfy a constraint C, unless each candidate that fares better than D on C also fares worse than D on some constraint that is higher ranked than C.

Harmonic ordering can be illustrated with CVT by reexamining the tableau in table 1.1 under the assumption that the universal constraints are ranked by a particular grammar, L_1, with the ranking given in (2.11).

(2.11)   Constraint hierarchy for L_1:
ONSET ≫ NOCODA ≫ FILL^{Nuc} ≫ PARSE ≫ FILL^{Ons}

The constraints (and their columns) are ordered in table 2.1 left to right, reflecting the hierarchy in (2.11). The candidates in this tableau have been listed in harmonic order, from highest to lowest Harmony; the optimal candidate is marked manually[4]. Starting at the bottom of the tableau, (a) < (c) can be verified as follows. The first step is to cancel common marks: here, there are none. The next step is to determine which candidate has the worst uncanceled mark—that is, most violates the most highly ranked constraint: it is (a), which violates ONSET. Therefore (a) is the less harmonic. In determining that (c) < (b), first cancel the common mark *PARSE; (c) then earns the worst remaining mark of the two, *FILL^{Nuc}. When comparing (b) to (d), one *PARSE mark cancels, leaving *marks'*(b) = {*PARSE} and *marks'*(d) = {*FILL^{Ons}}. The worst mark is the uncanceled *PARSE incurred by (b), so (b) < (d).

L_1 is a language in which all syllables have the overt form .CV.: onsets are required, codas are forbidden. In case of problematic inputs such as /VCVC/ where a faithful parse into CV syllables is not possible, this lan-

Table 2.4
Constraint tableau for L_2

Candidates		ONSET	NOCODA	FILL^{Ons}	PARSE	FILL^{Nuc}
/VCVC/ →						
☞ (c) ⟨V⟩.CV.C□́.					*	*
(b) ⟨V⟩.CV.⟨C⟩					* *	
(d) .□V.CV.⟨C⟩				*	*	
(a) .V.CVC.		*	*			

guage uses overparsing (of consonants) to provide missing onsets for vowels, and underparsing (of consonants) to avoid codas (it is the language denoted $\Sigma^{CV}_{ep,del}$ in P&S section 6.2.2.2).

Exchanging the two FILL constraints in L_1 gives the grammar L_2.

(2.12)   Constraint hierarchy for L_2:
ONSET ≫ NOCODA ≫ FILL^{Ons} ≫ PARSE ≫ FILL^{Nuc}

Now the tableau corresponding to table 2.1 becomes table 2.4; the columns have been reordered to reflect the constraint reranking, and the candidates have been reordered to reflect the new harmonic ordering.

Like L_1, all syllables in L_2 are CV; /VCVC/ gets syllabified differently, however. In L_2, underparsing (of vowels) is used to avoid onsetless syllables, and overparsing (of vowels) to avoid codas (L_2 is P&S's language $\Sigma^{CV}_{del,ep}$).

The relation between L_1 and L_2 illustrates a principle of OT central to learnability concerns.

(2.13)   *Typology by reranking*: Systematic crosslinguistic variation is due entirely to variation in language-specific total rankings of the universal constraints in *Con*. Analysis of the optimal forms arising from all possible total rankings of *Con* gives the typology of possible human languages. UG may impose restrictions on the possible rankings of *Con*.

Analysis of all rankings of the CVT constraints reveals a typology of basic CV syllable structures that explains Jakobson's typological generalizations (Jakobson 1962, Clements and Keyser 1983): see P&S chapter 6. In this typology, licit syllables may have required or optional onsets, and, independently, forbidden or optional codas.

These principles may also be illustrated with the GSL theory. To begin, Mark Cancelation is illustrated in table 2.5.

Harmonic ordering can be illustrated with GSL by reexamining the tableau in table 2.3, reproduced here as table 2.6, under the assumption that the universal constraints are ranked by a particular grammar of a language L_1' with the ranking given in (2.14). (This is a language like English with respect to the distribution of subjects.)

(2.14)   Constraint hierarchy for (English-like) L_1':
PARSE ≫ SUBJ ≫ FULL-INT ≫ DROP-TOP ≫ AL-FOC

The constraints are ordered in table 2.6 left to right, reflecting the hierarchy in (2.14). The candidates in this tableau have been listed in harmonic order, from highest to lowest Harmony. Starting at the bottom of the tableau, (a) < (c) can be verified as follows. The first step is to cancel common marks: here, *SUBJ. Then (c) has an uncanceled *DROP-TOP mark, $marks'(c) = \{*DROP\text{-}TOP\}$, while a has an uncanceled *PARSE mark, $marks'(a) = \{*PARSE\}$; so (a) is less harmonic. Next we verify that (c) < (d): the uncanceled mark of (c), *SUBJ, is assessed by a constraint that is higher ranked in L_1 than that assessing the uncanceled mark of (d), FULL-INT. Finally, (d) < (b) holds because (d) has an uncanceled mark while (b) does not.

As shown in the tableau in table 2.6, L_1 is a language in which unfocused topic-referring subjects are parsed into subject position (SpecIP). This English-like behavior changes to Italian-like behavior when the ranking of PARSE and SUBJ are lowered to their positions in the ranking defining language L_2'.

(2.15)   Constraint hierarchy for (Italian-like) L_2':
FULL-INT ≫ DROP-TOP ≫ PARSE ≫ AL-FOC ≫ SUBJ

As shown in the tableau of table 2.7, now an unfocused topic-referring subject is not parsed.

Analysis of all rankings of the GSL constraints derives a typology of subject distribution relating the presence or absence of expletive subjects, the preverbal or postverbal positioning of focused subjects, and the presence or absence of topic-referring subjects (see Grimshaw and Samek-Lodovici 1995, 1998; Samek-Lodovici 1996).

A final central principle of OT is given in (2.16).

Table 2.5
Mark Cancelation

⟨sing(x), x = topic, x = he; T = pres perf⟩	PARSE	SUBJ	FULL-INT	DROP-TOP	AL-FOC
☞ (b) [IP he_i has [t_i sung]]		*		⊠	
(c) [IP has [[t_i sung] he_i]]				⊠	

Table 2.6
Constraint tableau for (English-like) L'_1

⟨sing(x), x=topic, x=he; T=pres perf⟩	PARSE	SUBJ	FULL-INT	DROP-TOP	AL-FOC
☞ (b) [IP he_i has [t_i sung]]		*			
(d) [IP it has [[t_i sung] he_i]]			*	*	
(c) [IP has [[t_i sung] he_i]]		*		*	
(a) [IP has [sung]]	*	*		*	

Table 2.7
Constraint tableau for (Italian-like) L'_2

⟨sing(x), x = topic, x = he; T = pres perf⟩	FULL-INT	DROP-TOP	PARSE	AL-FOC	SUBJ
☞ (a) [IP has [sung]]					*
(b) [IP he_i has [t_i sung]]		*	*		
(c) [IP has [[t_i sung] he_i]]		*		*	
(d) [IP it has [[t_i sung] he_i]]	*	*			

(2.16) *Richness of the base*: The set of possible inputs to the grammars of all languages is the same. The grammatical inventories of languages are defined as the forms appearing in the outputs that emerge from the grammar when it is fed the universal set of all possible inputs (P&S section 9.3).

Systematic differences in inventories arise from different constraint rankings, not different inputs. The lexicon of a language is a sample from the inventory of possible inputs; all systematic properties of the lexicon arise indirectly from the grammar, that delimits the inventory from which the lexicon is drawn. There are no morpheme structure constraints on phonological inputs; no lexical parameter that determines whether a language has *pro*. In language L_1, all syllables have the form .CV. not because the possible *inputs* are restricted ahead of time to consist only of forms with strict CV alternation, but because the grammar so restricts the *outputs*. Richness of the base extends this style of explanation to all inventory phenomena. If any language lacks a particular structure, it is because any input containing the structure will have, as its optimal candidate, a structural description with an output that does not contain that structure: the optimal candidate will always change it into something else.

As our last issue concerning OT fundamentals, we return to the question of infinity. In the CVT, and quite typically in OT phonology, at least, $Gen(I)$ contains an infinite number of candidate structural descriptions of each input I. In the face of this infinity, is the theory well defined? Of course, the overwhelming majority of formal systems in mathematics involve an infinity of structures; the mere fact of infinity means only that the most primitive conceivable method, listing all the possibilities and checking each one, is infeasible. But even in finite cases, this method is commonly infeasible anyway. For an OT grammar to be well defined, it must be that for any input, which structure is optimal is formally determinate. The necessary formal definitions are provided in P&S chapter 5. To show that a given structure is the optimal parse of I, we need to provide a proof that none of the (infinitely many) other parses in $Gen(I)$ has higher Harmony. A general technique for such demonstration, the *Method of Mark Eliminability* (P&S section 7.3), proceeds by showing that any attempt to avoid the marks incurred by the putatively optimal output leads to alternatives that incur worse marks.[5]

Thus the infinite candidate set has a perfectly well-defined optimum (or optima, if multiple outputs incur exactly the same, optimal, set of marks). Yet it might still be the case that the task of actually computing the optimal candidate cannot be performed efficiently. But as Tesar (1995, 1996) has shown, computational feasibility is not a problem either, at least in the general cases studied to date. One reason is that the infinity of candidates derives from the unbounded potential for empty structure. But empty structure is always penalized by constraints of the FILL family: these militate against empty syllable positions in phonology (FILL^{Ons}, FILL^{Nuc}), empty X^0 positions in syntax (OBLIGATORY-HEADS of Grimshaw 1993, 1997), uninterpretable elements (FULL-INT), and the like. Optimal structures may have empty structure, in violation of FILL, only when that is necessary to avoid violation of higher-ranking constraints. This will not be the case for unbounded quantities of empty structure. It follows that finite inputs will only have a finite number of structural descriptions that are potentially optimal, under some constraint ranking. Thus a parser constructing an optimal parse of a given input I need only have access to a finite part of the infinite space $Gen(I)$.

The parsing algorithms developed by Tesar construct optimal parses from increasingly large portions of the input, requiring an amount of computational time and storage space that grows with the size of the input only as fast as for parsers of conventional, rewrite-rule grammars of corresponding complexity. The structure in the space of candidates allows for efficient computation of optimal parses, even though the grammar's specification of well-formedness makes reference to an infinite set of parses.

2.3   The Grammar Learning Problem

Having provided the necessary principles, we can now insert the crucial grammatical structure of OT into the learning problem schematically formulated in section 1.3.

(2.17)   Our grammar learning problem (including relevant grammatical structure).

Given: Learning data in the form of full grammatical structural
          descriptions.
          The universal components of any OT grammar:

    · The set of possible inputs
    · The function *Gen* generating the candidate outputs for any
    possible input
    · The constraints *Con* on well-formedness

Find: a language-particular OT grammar, consisting of a ranking
    (or set of rankings) of the constraints in *Con*, consistent with
    all the given data.

The initial data for the learning problem are well-formed candidate structural descriptions; each consists of an input together with the output declared optimal by the target grammar. For example, the learner of the CV language L_1 might have as an initial datum .☐V.CV.⟨C⟩, candidate (d) of table 2.1, the parse assigned to the input $I = $ /VCVC/; the learner of the Italian-like language L_2' might have as an initial datum the input $I = $ ⟨sing(x), x = topic, x = he; T = pres perf⟩ together with its grammatical parse, $p = [_{IP}$ has [sung]] of table 2.7(a).

3 Constraint Demotion

3.1 The Principle of Constraint Demotion

Optimality Theory is inherently comparative; the grammaticality of a structural description is determined not in isolation, but with respect to competing candidates. Therefore, the learner is not informed about the correct ranking by positive data in isolation; the role of the competing candidates must be addressed. This fact is not a liability, but an advantage: a comparative theory gives comparative structure to be exploited. Each piece of positive evidence, a grammatical structural description, brings with it a body of implicit negative evidence in the form of the competing descriptions. Given access to *Gen* (which is universal) and the underlying form (contained in the given structural description), the learner has access to these competitors. Any competing candidate, along with the grammatical structure, determines a data pair related to the correct ranking: the correct ranking must make the grammatical structure more harmonic than the ungrammatical competitor.

This can be stated more concretely in the context of Basic CV Syllable Theory. Suppose the learner receives a piece of explicit positive evidence like $p = .\square V.CV.\langle C \rangle$. Now consider any other parse of p's input $I = $ /VCVC/; e.g., $p' = .V.CVC$. In the general case, there are two possibilities. Either an alternative parse p' has exactly the same marks as p, in which case p' has the same Harmony as p (no matter what the unknown ranking) and must be tied for optimality: p' too then is a grammatical parse of I. This case is unusual, but possible. In the typical case, a competitor p' and p will not have identical marks. In this case the harmonic ordering of forms determined by the unknown ranking will declare one more harmonic than the other; it must be p that is the more harmonic, since it is given as well-formed learning data and is thus optimal.

For each well-formed example p a learner receives, therefore, every other parse p' of the same input must be suboptimal—that is, ill formed—unless p' happens to have exactly the same marks as p. Thus a single positive example, a parse p of an input I, conveys a body of implicit negative evidence: all the other parses p' in $Gen(I)$—with the exception of those parses that the learner can recognize as tied for optimality with p in virtue of having the same marks.

In our CV example, a learner given the positive datum $p = .\square V.CV.\langle C \rangle$ knows that, with respect to the unknown constraint hierarchy of the language being learned, the alternative parse of the same input, $p' = $ .V.CVC., is less harmonic:

(3.1)   .V.CVC. < .□V.CV.⟨C⟩

Furthermore, corresponding harmonic comparisons must hold for every other parse p'' in *Gen*(/VCVC/).

The implicit negative evidence provided by the structure of OT can also be illustrated with the GSL theory. Suppose the learner receives a piece of explicit positive evidence such as the form: $p = $ ⟨sing(x), x = topic, x = he; T = pres perf⟩; [$_{IP}$ has [sung]]. (Recall that in OT, full structural descriptions consist of an "input", an "output", and a correspondence between their elements. This example informs the learner that an unfocused, topic-referring subject is not overtly realized in the target language.) Now consider any other parse p' of p's input $I = $ ⟨sing(x), x = topic, x = he; T = pres perf⟩; e.g., the parse p' with output [$_{IP}$ he$_i$ has [t$_i$ sung]]. Having received the positive datum p, the learner knows that, with respect to the unknown constraint hierarchy of the language being learned, the alternative parse of the same input, p', is less harmonic:

(3.2)   for $I = $ ⟨sing(x), x = topic, x = he; T = pres perf⟩,   [$_{IP}$ he$_i$ has [t$_i$ sung]] < [$_{IP}$ has [sung]].

Thus each single piece of positive initial data conveys a large amount of inferred comparative data of the form outlined in (3.3).

(3.3)   [suboptimal parse of input I, "*loser*"] < [optimal parse of input I, "*winner*"]

Such pairs are what feed our learning algorithm. Each pair carries the information that the constraints violated by the suboptimal parse loser must outrank those violated by the optimal parse winner. That is, in some sense, we must have *marks*(*loser*) ≫ *marks*(*winner*).

(3.4)   The key: *loser-marks* ≫ *winner-marks*

The learning procedure we now develop is nothing but a way of making this observation precise and deducing its consequences. The challenge faced by the learner is: given a suitable set of such *loser/winner pairs*, to find a ranking such that each *winner* is more harmonic than its corresponding *loser*. Constraint Demotion solves this challenge, by demoting the constraints violated by the winner down in the hierarchy so that they are dominated by the constraints violated by the loser.

3.1.1 The Basic Idea

In our CV language L_1, the winner for input /VCVC/ is .□V.CV.⟨C⟩. Table 2.1 gave the marks incurred by the winner (labeled (d)) and by three competing losers. These may be used to form three *loser/winner* pairs, as shown in table 3.1. A *mark-data pair* is the paired lists of constraint violation marks for a *loser/winner* pair.

To make contact with more familiar OT constraint tableaux, the information in table 3.1 will also be displayed in the format of table 3.2.

At this point, the constraints are unranked; the dotted vertical lines separating constraints in table 3.2 convey that no relative ranking of adjacent constraints is intended. The winner is indicated with a ✓; ☞ will denote the structure that is optimal according to the current grammar, which may not be the same as the winner (the structure that is grammatical in the target language). The constraint violations of the winner,

Table 3.1
Mark-data pairs (L_1)

	loser	≺	winner	marks(loser)	marks(winner)
(a) ≺ (d)	.V.CVC.	≺	.□V.CV.⟨C⟩	*ONSET *NOCODA	*PARSE *FILL^{Ons}
(b) ≺ (d)	⟨V⟩.CV.⟨C⟩	≺	.□V.CV.⟨C⟩	*PARSE *PARSE	*PARSE *FILL^{Ons}
(c) ≺ (d)	⟨V⟩.CV.C□.	≺	.□V.CV.⟨C⟩	*PARSE *FILL^{Nuc}	*PARSE *FILL^{Ons}

Table 3.2
Initial data

loser/winner pairs	not-yet-ranked				
	FILL^{Nuc}	FILL^{Ons}	PARSE	ONSET	NOCODA
(d) ✓ .□V.CV.⟨C⟩		⊛	⊛		
(a) .V.CVC.				*	*
(d) ✓ .□V.CV.⟨C⟩		⊛	⊗		
(b) ⟨V⟩.CV.⟨C⟩			*		
(d) ✓ .□V.CV.⟨C⟩		⊛	⊗		
(c) ⟨V⟩.CV.C □.	*		✕		

Table 3.3
Mark-data pairs after cancelation (L_1)

loser/winner pairs				marks'(loser)	marks'(winner)
(a) ≺ (d)	.V.CVC.	≺	.□V.CV.⟨C⟩	*ONSET *NOCODA	*PARSE *FILL^Ons
(b) ≺ (d)	⟨V⟩.CV.⟨C⟩	≺	.□V.CV.⟨C⟩	~~*PARSE~~ *PARSE	~~*PARSE~~ *FILL^Ons
(c) ≺ (d)	⟨V⟩.CV.C□.	≺	.□V.CV.⟨C⟩	~~*PARSE~~ *FILL^Nuc	~~*PARSE~~ *FILL^Ons

marks(*winner*), are distinguished by the symbol ⊛. Mark cancelation is denoted by diagonal crossing, as in table 2.3.

In order that each loser be less harmonic than the winner, the marks incurred by the former, *marks*(*loser*), must collectively be worse than *marks*(*winner*). According to (2.9), what this means more precisely is that *loser* must incur the worst uncanceled mark, compared to *winner*. This requires that uncanceled marks be identified, so the first step is to cancel the common marks in table 3.1, as shown in table 3.3.

The canceled marks have been ~~struck out~~. Note that the cancelation operation that transforms *marks* to *marks'* is defined only on pairs of sets of marks—for example, *PARSE is canceled in the pairs (b) < (d) and (c) < (d), but not in the pair (a) < (d). Note also that cancelation of marks is done token by token: in the row (b) < (d), one but not the other mark *PARSE in *marks*(b) is canceled.

The mark-data after cancelation are the data on which Constraint Demotion operates. The representation in tableau form, given in table 3.2, reveals what successful learning must accomplish: the ranking of the constraints must be adjusted so that, for each pair, all the uncanceled winner marks ⊛ are dominated by at least one loser mark *. Using the standard tableau convention of positioning the highest-ranked constraints to the left, the columns containing uncanceled ⊛ (winner marks) need to be moved far enough to the right (down in the hierarchy) so that, for each pair, there is a column (constraint) containing an uncanceled * (loser mark) further to the left (dominant in the hierarchy) than all the columns containing uncanceled ⊛ (winner marks).

The algorithm to accomplish this is based on the principle in (3.5).

(3.5)   *Principle of Constraint Demotion*: For any constraint ℂ assessing an uncanceled winner mark, if ℂ is not dominated by a constraint assessing an uncanceled loser mark, demote ℂ to immediately below the highest-ranked constraint assessing an uncanceled loser mark.

Constraint Demotion works by demoting the constraints with un-canceled winner marks down far enough in the hierarchy so that they are dominated by a constraint with an uncanceled loser mark, ensuring that each winner is more harmonic than its competing losers.

Notice that it is not necessary for *all* uncanceled loser marks to dom-inate all uncanceled winner marks: one will suffice. However, given more than one uncanceled loser mark, it is often not immediately apparent which one needs to dominate the uncanceled winner marks (the pair (a) $\prec$ (d) above is such a case). This is the challenge successfully overcome by Constraint Demotion.

3.1.2 Stratified Domination Hierarchies

OT grammars are defined by rankings in which the domination rela-tion between any two constraints is specified. The learning algorithm, however, works with a larger space of hypotheses, the space of stratified hierarchies. A stratified domination hierarchy has the form in (3.6).

(3.6)   Stratified domination hierarchy
$$\{C_1, C_2, \ldots, C_3\} \gg \{C_4, C_5, \ldots, C_6\} \gg \ldots \gg \{C_7, C_8, \ldots, C_9\}$$

The constraints $C_1, C_2, \ldots, C_3$ comprise the first stratum in the hier-archy: they are not ranked with respect to one another, but they each dominate all the remaining constraints. Similarly, the constraints $C_4, C_5,$ $\ldots, C_6$ comprise the second stratum: they are not ranked with respect to one another, but they each dominate all the constraints in the lower strata. In tableaux, strata will be separated from each other by solid ver-tical lines, while constraints within the same stratum will be separated by dotted lines, with no relative ranking implied.

The original notion of constraint ranking, in which a domination rela-tion is specified for every pair of candidates, can now be seen as a special case of the stratified hierarchy, where each stratum contains exactly one constraint. That special case will be labeled here a total ranking. Hence-forth, "hierarchy" will mean stratified hierarchy; when appropriate, hier-archies will be explicitly qualified as "totally ranked".

The definition of harmonic ordering (2.9) needs to be elaborated slightly for stratified hierarchies. When C_1 and C_2 are in the same

Table 3.4
Harmonic ordering with a stratified hierarchy: $\mathbb{C}_1 \gg \{\mathbb{C}_2, \mathbb{C}_3\} \gg \mathbb{C}_4$

	$\mathbb{C}_1$	$\mathbb{C}_2$	$\mathbb{C}_3$	$\mathbb{C}_4$
p_1	*!		*	
p_2			*	*!
☞ p_3		*		
p_4			* *!	

stratum, two marks $*\mathbb{C}_1$ and $*\mathbb{C}_2$ are equally weighted in the computation of Harmony. In effect, all constraints in a single stratum are collapsed together, and treated as though they were a single constraint, for the purposes of determining the relative Harmony of candidates. Minimal violation with respect to a stratum is determined by the candidate incurring the smallest sum of violations assessed by all constraints in the stratum. The tableau in table 3.4 gives a simple illustration.

Here, all candidates are compared to the optimal one, p_3. In this illustration, parses p_2 and p_3 violate different constraints, which are in the same stratum of the hierarchy. Therefore, these marks cannot decide between the candidates, and it is left to the lower-ranked constraint to decide in favor of p_3. Notice that candidate p_4 is still eliminated by the middle stratum because it incurs more than the minimal number of marks to constraints in the middle stratum. (The symbol *! indicates a mark fatal in comparison with the optimal parse.)

With respect to the comparison of candidates, marks assessed by different constraints in the same stratum can be thought of as "canceling", because they do not decide between the candidates. It is crucial, though, that the marks not be canceled for the purposes of learning. The term *Mark Cancelation*, as used in the rest of this book, should be understood to only cancel marks assessed by the same constraint to competing candidates; this is valid independent of the target constraint hierarchy, which, during learning, is unknown.

3.1.3   An Example: Basic CV Syllable Theory

Constraint Demotion (abbreviated CD) will now be illustrated using CVT—specifically, with the target language L_1 of table 2.1 and (2.11). The initial stratified hierarchy is set to

(3.7) $\mathcal{H} = \mathcal{H}_0 = \{$FILL^{Nuc}, FILL^{Ons}, PARSE, ONSET, NOCODA$\}$

Suppose that the first loser/winner pair is (b) $\prec$ (d) of table 3.1. Mark Cancelation is applied to the corresponding pair of mark lists, resulting in the mark-data pair shown in table 3.5.

Now CD can be applied. The highest ranked (in $\mathcal{H}$) uncanceled loser mark—the only one—is *PARSE. The *marks'*(winner) are checked to see if they are dominated by *PARSE. The only winner mark is *FILL^{Ons}, which is *not* so dominated. CD therefore calls for demoting FILL^{Ons} to the stratum immediately below PARSE. Since no such stratum currently exists, it is created. The resulting hierarchy is (3.8).

(3.8) $\mathcal{H} = \{$FILL^{Nuc}, PARSE, ONSET, NOCODA$\} \gg \{$FILL$^{\text{Ons}}\}$

This demotion is shown in tableau form in table 3.6; recall that strata are separated by solid vertical lines, whereas dotted vertical lines separate constraints in the same stratum. The uncanceled winner mark ⊛ is demoted to a (new) stratum immediately below the stratum containing the highest uncanceled winner mark *, which now becomes a fatal violation *! rendering irrelevant the dominated violation (which is therefore grayed out).

Now another loser/winner pair is selected. Suppose this is (a) $\prec$ (d) of table 3.1, as shown in table 3.7.

Table 3.5
Mark-data pair, step 1 (L_1)

	loser	$\prec$	winner	marks'(loser)	marks'(winner)
(b) $\prec$ (d)	$\langle$V$\rangle$.CV.$\langle$C$\rangle$	$\prec$	.□V.CV.$\langle$C$\rangle$	*PARSE *PARSE	*PARSE FILL^{Ons}

Table 3.6
First demotion

loser/winner pair		FILL^{Nuc}	FILL^{Ons}	PARSE	ONSET	NOCODA	FILL^{Ons}
(d) ✓☞	.□V.CV.$\langle$C$\rangle$		⊛	✗			⊛
(b)	$\langle$V$\rangle$.CV. $\langle$C$\rangle$			✗ *!			

Table 3.7
Mark-data pair for CD, step 2 (L_1)

	loser ≺ winner		marks'(loser)	marks'(winner)
(a) ≺ (d)	.V.CVC.	≺	.□V.CV.⟨C⟩	*ONSET *NOCODA	*PARSE *FILL^{Ons}

Table 3.8
Second demotion

loser/winner pair		FILL^{Nuc}	PARSE	ONSET	NOCODA	FILL^{Ons}	PARSE
(d) ✓☞	.□V.CV.⟨C⟩		⊛			⊛	⊛
(a)	.V.CVC.			*!	*!		

Table 3.9
Mark-data pair for CD, step 3 (L_1)

	loser ≺ winner		marks'(loser)	marks'(winner)
(c) ≺ (d)	⟨V⟩.CV.C□.	≺	.□V.CV.⟨C⟩	~~*PARSE~~ *FILL^{Nuc}	~~*PARSE~~ *FILL^{Ons}

There are no common marks to cancel. CD calls for finding the
highest-ranked of the *marks'(loser)*. Since ONSET and NOCODA are both
top ranked, either will do; choose, say, ONSET. Next, each constraint with
a mark in *marks'(winner)* is checked to see if it is dominated by ONSET.
FILL^{Ons} is so dominated. PARSE is not, however, so it is demoted to the
stratum immediately below that of ONSET.

(3.9) $\mathcal{H} = \{$FILL^{Ons}, ONSET, NOCODA$\} \gg \{$FILL^{Ons}, PARSE$\}$

In tableau form, this demotion is shown in table 3.8. (Both the ONSET
and NOCODA violations are marked as fatal, *!, because both are highest-
ranking violations of the loser: they belong to the same stratum.)

Suppose now that the next *loser/winner* pair is as shown in table 3.9.

Since the uncanceled loser mark, *FILL^{Nuc}, already dominates the
uncanceled winner mark, *FILL^{Ons}, no demotion results, and $\mathcal{H}$ is unchanged. This is an example of an *uninformative* pair, given its location
in the sequence of training pairs: no demotions result.

Table 3.10
Mark-data pair for CD, step 4 (L_1)

loser	≺	winner	marks'(loser)	marks'(winner)
⟨VC⟩	≺	.□V.⟨C⟩	~~*PARSE~~ *PARSE	~~*PARSE~~ *FILL^{Ons}

Table 3.11
Third demotion

loser/winner pair	FILL^{Nuc}	ONSET	NOCODA	FILL^{Ons}	PARSE	FILL^{Ons}
✓☞ .□V.⟨C⟩				⊛		⊛
⟨VC⟩					*!	

Suppose the next *loser/winner* pair results from a new input, /VC/, with a new optimal parse, .□V.⟨C⟩, as shown in table 3.10.

Since the winner mark * FILL^{Ons} is not dominated by the loser mark *PARSE, it must be demoted to the stratum immediately below PARSE, resulting in the hierarchy in (3.10).

(3.10)   ℋ = {FILL^{Nuc}, ONSET, NOCODA} ≫ {PARSE} ≫ {FILL^{Ons}}

This demotion is shown in table 3.11.

This stratified hierarchy generates precisely L_1, using the interpretation of stratified hierarchies described above. For any further *loser/winner* pairs that could be considered, *loser* is guaranteed to have at least one uncanceled mark assessed by a constraint dominating all the constraints assessing uncanceled marks to *winner*. Thus, no further data will be informative: L_1 has been learned.

A parallel example could be developed using the GSL theory. An example of a demotion step resulting from the loser/winner pair of (27) is shown in table 3.12. Prior to demotion, all constraints are unranked. With respect to this stratified hierarchy, the loser (b) is more harmonic than the desired winner (a), an error. The two uncanceled winner marks (assessed by SUBJ and PARSE) must be demoted to a stratum just below that of the sole loser mark, *DROP-TOP. This requires creation of such a stratum; after demotion, the learner's stratified hierarchy has two strata (separated by the heavy vertical line).

Table 3.12
Constraint Demotion for (Italian-like) L'_2

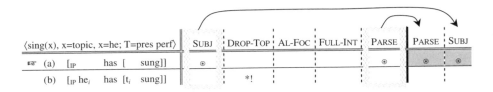

⟨sing(x), x=topic, x=he; T=pres perf⟩	SUBJ	DROP-TOP	AL-FOC	FULL-INT	PARSE	PARSE	SUBJ
☞ (a) [IP has [sung]]	⊛					⊛	⊛	⊛
(b) [IP he$_i$ has [t$_i$ sung]]		*!					

Table 3.13
The disjunction problem

loser/winner pair	FILL^{Ons}	ONSET	FILL^{Nuc}	NOCODA	PARSE
(a) V.CVC.		*		*	
(d) ☞ .□V.CV.⟨C⟩	⊛				⊛

3.1.4 Why Not Constraint Promotion?

Constraint Demotion is defined entirely in terms of *demotion*; all movement of constraints is downward in the hierarchy. One could reasonably ask if this is an arbitrary choice; couldn't the learner just as easily promote constraints toward the correct hierarchy? The answer is no, and understanding why reveals the logic behind Constraint Demotion.

Consider the tableau shown in table 3.13, with (d) the winner and (a) the loser. The ranking depicted in the tableau makes the loser, (a), more harmonic than the winner, (d), so the learner needs to change the hierarchy to achieve the desired result, (a) < (d).

There are no marks in common, so no marks are canceled. For the winner to be more harmonic than the loser, at least one of the loser's marks must dominate all the winner's marks. This relation is expressed in (3.11).

(3.11)   (ONSET or NOCODA) ≫ (FILL^{Ons} and PARSE)

Demotion moves the constraints corresponding to the winner's marks. They are contained in a conjunction (*and*); thus, once the highest-ranked loser mark is identified, *all* the winner marks need to be dominated by it, so all constraints with winner marks are demoted if not already so dominated. A hypothetical *promotion* operation would move the constraints corresponding to the *loser's* marks up in the hierarchy. But notice that the loser's marks are contained in a *disjunction* (*or*). It is not clear which of the loser's violations should be promoted; perhaps all of them, or perhaps just one. Other data might require one of the constraints violated by the loser to be dominated by one of the constraints violated by the winner. This *loser/winner* pair gives no basis for choosing.

Disjunctions are notoriously problematic in general computational learning theory. Constraint Demotion solves the problem of disentangling the disjunctions by demoting the constraints violated by the winner; there is no choice to be made among them—all must be dominated. The choice between the constraints violated by the loser is made by picking the one highest ranked in the current hierarchy (in table 3.13, that is ONSET). Thus, if other data have already determined that ONSET ≫ NOCODA, that relationship is preserved. The constraints violated by the winner are only demoted as far as necessary.

3.2 Analysis of Constraint Demotion

3.2.1 Learnability Results: Convergence and Efficiency

The illustration of Constraint Demotion given in section 3.1.3 started with initial hierarchy $\mathcal{H}_0$, given in (3.7), having all the constraints in one stratum. Using this initial hierarchy is convenient for demonstrating some formal properties. By starting with all constraints at the top, CD can be understood to demote constraints down toward their correct position. Because CD only demotes constraints as far as necessary, a constraint never gets demoted below its target position, and will not be demoted further once reaching its target position. The formal analysis that assumes $\mathcal{H}_0$ as the initial hierarchy proves the following results.

(3.12) THEOREM Correctness of Constraint Demotion (initial hierarchy $\mathcal{H}_0$)
Starting with all constraints in *Con* ranked in the top stratum, and applying Constraint Demotion to informative positive evidence as long as such exists, the process converges on a stratified hierarchy such that all totally ranked refinements of that hierarchy correctly account for the learning data.

(3.13) THEOREM   Data complexity of Constraint Demotion (initial hierarchy $\mathcal{H}_0$)
Starting with all constraints in *Con* ranked in the top stratum, the number of informative data pairs required for learning is at most $N(N - 1)/2$, where N is the number of constraints in *Con*.

The data complexity of a learning algorithm is the amount of data that needs to be supplied to the algorithm to ensure that it learns the correct grammar. For Constraint Demotion, each informative data pair results in a demotion, and the convergence results ensure that each demotion brings the hypothesized grammar ever closer to the correct grammar. Therefore, it is convenient to measure data complexity in terms of the maximum number of informative data pairs needed before the correct grammar is reached.

In Constraint Demotion, an informative pair can result in the demotion of one or several constraints, each being demoted down one or more strata. The minimum amount of progress resulting from a single error is the demotion of one constraint down one stratum. The worst-case data complexity thus amounts to the maximum distance between a possible starting hierarchy and a possible target hierarchy to be learned, where the distance between the two hierarchies is measured in terms of one-stratum demotions of constraints. The maximum possible distance between the initial hierarchy $\mathcal{H}_0$ and a target hierarchy is $N(N - 1)/2$, where N is the number of constraints in the grammar; this then is the maximum number of informative data pairs needed to learn the correct hierarchy.

The significance of this result is perhaps best illustrated by comparing it to the number of possible grammars. Given that any target grammar is consistent with at least one total ranking of the constraints, the number of possible grammars is potentially as large as the number of possible total rankings, $N!$. This number grows very quickly as a function of the number of constraints N, and if the amount of data required for learning scaled with the number of possible total rankings, it would be cause for concern indeed. Fortunately, the data complexity of CD is quite reasonable in its scaling. In fact, it does not take many universal constraints to give a drastic difference between the data complexity of CD and the number of total rankings: when $N = 10$, the CD data complexity is 45, while the number of total rankings is over 3.6 million. With 20 constraints, the CD data complexity is 190, while the number of total rankings is over 2 billion billion (2.43×10^{18}). This reveals the restrictiveness of the structure imposed by OT on the space of grammars: a learner can efficiently home in on any target grammar, managing an explosively sized grammar space with quite modest data requirements by fully exploiting the inherent structure provided by strict domination.

The power provided by strict domination for learning can be further underscored by considering that CD uses as its working hypothesis space not the space of total rankings, but the space of all stratified hierarchies, which is much larger and contains all total rankings as a subset. The disparity between the size of the working hypothesis space and the actual data requirements is that much greater.

As argued in chapter 1, the number of grammars made available by a grammatical framework is a rather crude measure of its explanatory power. A more significant measure is the degree to which the *structure* of UG allows rich grammars to be learned with realistically few positive examples. The crude number-of-grammars measure may be the best one can do given a theory of UG that does not enable the better learnability measure to be determined. In OT, however, we do have a quantitative and formally justified measure of learnability available in our $N(N-1)/2$ limit on the number of informative examples needed to solve our grammar learning problem. And we can see precisely how large the discrepancy can be between the number of grammars made available by a UG and the efficiency of learning that its structure enables.

This dramatic difference between the size of the OT grammar space and the number of informative examples needed to learn a grammar is due to the well-structured character of the space of fully ranked constraint hierarchies. It is useful to consider a set of parameters in the grammar space that suffice to specify the $N!$ grammars: these parameters state, for each pair of different constraints C_i and C_j, which is dominant—that is, whether $C_i \gg C_j$ or $C_j \gg C_i$. There are in fact $N(N-1)/2$ such dominance parameters,[1] and this is the maximum number of informative examples needed to learn a correct hierarchy when starting from the $\mathcal{H}_0$ initial hierarchy.[2] Efficient learning via Constraint Demotion is possible because the enlarged hypothesis space allows these dominance parameters to be unspecified (in the initial state, they are *all* unspecified), and because evidence for adjusting these dominance parameters can be assessed independently (via the key idea (3.4): *loser-marks* ≫ *winner-marks*). A single adjustment may not irrevocably set a correct value for any dominance parameter, each adjustment brings the hierarchy closer to the target, and eventually the adjustments are guaranteed to produce a correct set of parameter values. Note that what is independently adjustable here is not the substantive *content* of individual grammatical principles: it is the *interaction* of the principles, as determined by their relative rankings.

3.2.2   Arbitrary Initial Hierarchies

While the use of initial hierarchy $\mathcal{H}_0$ is convenient for purposes of illustration, it is by no means necessary for the success of Constraint Demotion. The formal proof of the correctness of Constraint Demotion can be extended to arbitrary initial constraint hierarchies, without any change whatsoever to the algorithm itself. Further, no significant change in the data complexity occurs: it is still a quadratic function of the number of constraints.

(3.14)   THEOREM   Correctness of Constraint Demotion
Starting with an arbitrary constraint hierarchy, and applying Constraint Demotion to informative positive evidence as long as such exists, the process converges on a stratified hierarchy such that all totally ranked refinements of that hierarchy correctly account for the learning data.

(3.15)   THEOREM   Data complexity of Constraint Demotion
Starting with an arbitrary constraint hierarchy, the number of informative data pairs required for learning is no more than $N(N-1)$, where N is the number of constraints in *Con*.

In fact, this upper bound is a significant overestimate, even more so than the one given for the special case with initial hierarchy $\mathcal{H}_0$.

With arbitrary initial hierarchies, CD can lead to empty strata; this can be seen as follows. Because the data observed must all be consistent with some total ranking, there is at least one constraint never assessing an uncanceled winner mark: the constraint top ranked in the total ranking. It is possible to have more than one such constraint (there are three for L_1); there will always be at least one. These constraints will never be demoted for any loser/winner pair, because only constraints assessing uncanceled winner marks for some loser/winner pair get demoted. Therefore, these constraints will stay put, no matter where they are in the initial hierarchy. If $\mathcal{H}_0$ is used, these constraints start at the top and stay there. For other initial hierarchies, these constraints stay put, and the other constraints eventually get demoted below them. This may leave some empty strata at the top, but that is of no consequence; all that matters is the relative position of the strata containing constraints.

Another learnability result now easily follows as well. In OT, a standard treatment of markedness scales is to posit in UG that certain constraints are universally ranked in a particular subhierarchy. For example, in P&S chapter 9, the markedness scale of place of articulation, according to which Coronal is less marked than, for example, Labial, is achieved via the UG requirement that the constraints violated by Cor(onal) and Lab(ial) PLace are universally ranked as in (3.16).

(3.16)   Coronal unmarkedness universal subhierarchy
          *PL/Lab $\gg$ *PL/Cor

In syntax, Legendre and others (Legendre et al. 1995; Legendre, Smolensky, and Wilson 1998) have proposed a universal hierarchy MɪɴLɪɴᴋ, which realizes the "Shortest Link" principle. We now see that having such UG rankings in the initial state does not jeopardize learnability. The Constraint Demotion algorithm is easily adapted so that whenever a constraint that is part of a universal markedness subhierarchy is demoted, the constraints below it in the hierarchy are also demoted if necessary to preserve the universal subhierarchy.

3.2.3   Learnability and Total Ranking

In this subsection we take up some rather subtle issues concerning the roles of fully ranked and stratified constraint hierarchies in these learning algorithms.

The discussion here assumes that the learning data are generated by a UG-allowed grammar, which, by (2.13), is a totally ranked hierarchy. When learning is successful, the learned stratified hierarchy, even if not totally ranked, is completely consistent with at least one total ranking. The empirical basis for (2.13) is the broad finding that correct typologies of adult languages do not seem to result when constraints are permitted to form stratified hierarchies. Generally speaking, allowing constraints to have equal ranking produces empirically problematic constraint interactions.

From the learnability perspective, the formal results given for Constraint Demotion depend critically on the assumption that the target language is given by a totally ranked hierarchy. This is a consequence of a principle implicit in CD. This principle states that the learner should assume that the observed description is optimal for the corresponding input, and that it is the *only* optimal description. This principle resembles other proposed learning principles, such as Clark's Principle of Contrast (Clark 1987) and Wexler's Uniqueness Principle (Wexler 1981). CD makes vigorous use of this learning principle.

When presented data from a non–totally ranked stratified hierarchy, it is in fact possible for CD to run endlessly. For the minimal illustration, suppose that there are two constraints $\mathbb{C}$ and $\mathbb{C}'$, and two candidate parses p and p', where p violates only $\mathbb{C}$ and p' violates only $\mathbb{C}'$. Suppose $\mathbb{C}$ and $\mathbb{C}'$ are both initially top ranked. Assume the target hierarchy also ranks $\mathbb{C}$ and $\mathbb{C}'$ in the same stratum, and that the two candidates tie for optimality. Both p and p' will therefore be separately observed as positive evidence. When p is observed, CD will assume the competitor p' to be suboptimal, since its marks are not identical to those of p. CD will therefore demote $\mathbb{C}$, the constraint violated by the observed optimal parse p, below $\mathbb{C}'$. Later, when the other optimal candidate p' is observed, CD will reverse the rankings of the constraints. This will continue endlessly, and learning will fail to converge. Notice that this instability occurs even though the initial hierarchy correctly had the constraints in the same stratum. Not only does the algorithm fail to converge on the non–fully ranked target hierarchy: when given the correct hierarchy, in time CD rejects it.

In understanding this somewhat unusual state of affairs, it is important to carefully distinguish the space of target grammars being learned from the space of hypotheses being explored during learning. Following the tenets of OT, we take the target grammars to be totally ranked hierarchies. Constraint Demotion does not operate within the confines of the space of totally ranked hierarchies, however. All evidence to date indicates that feasible learning of the target space requires a learning algorithm to search within a larger space: the space of stratified hierarchies. This is neither self-contradictory nor extremely unusual. In fact, it is consistent with a general theme of recent work in Computational Learning Theory (e.g., Pitt and Valiant 1988, Kearns and Vazirani 1994; for a tutorial, see Haussler 1996).

It is often assumed in learnability theory that language acquisition operates within the limits imposed by UG: that hypothesized grammars are always fully specified grammars admitted by UG. This assumption has the potential disadvantage that the hypotheses all involve full commitment with respect to dimensions of grammatical variation, even though no evidence may yet have been obtained to justify such commitments. The stratified hierarchies constituting the hypothesis space exploited by Constraint Demotion, by contrast, can be widely uncommitted on the relative ranking of constraints, useful when no relevant evidence has yet been observed. This is crucial to the successful operation of CD. On the other hand, the more traditional assumption that the learner's hypotheses are all UG-allowed grammars has the advantage that learning can never terminate in a UG-disallowed state; such a learning process makes it obvious why adult grammars lie in the UG-allowed space. In our case, since learning takes place in the larger space of stratified hierarchies, we must explicitly address two questions: How does the learner get to a UG-allowed grammar (a totally ranked hierarchy)? And why must adult grammars always be totally ranked hierarchies?

How does the learner get to a totally ranked hierarchy? At the endpoint of learning, the hierarchy may not be fully ranked: the result is a stratified hierarchy with the property that *any* further refinement into a fully ranked hierarchy will correctly account for all the learning data. Lacking any evidence on which to do so, the learning algorithm does not commit to any of these. In human terms, however, one could suppose that by adulthood, a learner has taken the learned stratified hierarchy and refined it to a fully ranked hierarchy. It is not clear that anything depends on which fully ranked hierarchy is chosen.

Why must adult grammars be totally ranked hierarchies? The situation we have described is a rather curious one. When learning data from a fully ranked hierarchy is presented to our learning algorithms, they generally terminate in a stratified hierarchy with the property that all of its refinements into totally ranked hierarchies correctly generate the learning data. But when the learning data derive from a non–totally ranked stratified hierarchy, the algorithms can fail to terminate at all. Thus the space of fully ranked hierarchies is learnable by Constraint Demotion followed by refinement to some (any) fully ranked hierarchy; the larger space of stratified hierarchies is not learnable via CD, as far as we can determine at this point.

It is currently an open question whether the Constraint Demotion approach can be extended to learn languages generated by stratified hierarchies in general, including those inconsistent with any total ranking. In such languages, some inputs may have multiple optimal outputs that do not earn identical sets of marks. In such a setting, the learner's primary data might consist of a set of underlying forms, and for each, *all* its optimal structural descriptions, should there be more than one. Much of the analysis might extend to this setting, but the algorithm would need to be extended with an additional step to handle pairs opt_1 ~ opt_2 of tying optima. In this step, each mark in $marks'(opt_1)$ must be placed in the same stratum as a corresponding mark in $marks'(opt_2)$: a somewhat delicate business. Indeed, achieving ties for optimality between forms that incur different marks is always a delicate matter. It appears likely to us that learning languages that do not derive from a totally ranked hierarchy is in general much more difficult than the totally ranked case. If this is indeed true, demands of learnability could ultimately explain a fundamental principle of OT: UG admits only (adult) grammars defined by totally ranked hierarchies.

While learnability appears to be problematic in the face of ties for optimality between outputs with *different* marks (impossible given a totally ranked hierarchy), CD has no problems whatever coping with ties for optimality between outputs with the *same* marks (possible given a totally ranked hierarchy): given two such outputs as a data pair, all marks cancel, and CD correctly leaves the hierarchy unchanged.

3.3   Error-Driven Constraint Demotion

Having developed the basic principle of Constraint Demotion, we now show how it can be incorporated into a procedure for learning a grammar from correct structural descriptions.

CD operates on loser/winner pairs, deducing consequences for the grammar from the fact that the winner must be more harmonic than the loser. The winner is a positive example provided externally to the grammar learner: a parse of some input (e.g., an underlying lexical form in phonology; a predicate/argument structure in syntax), a parse taken to be optimal according to the target grammar. The loser is an alternative parse of the same input, which must be suboptimal with respect to the target grammar (unless it happens to have exactly the same marks as the winner). Presumably, such a loser must be generated by the grammar learner. Whether the loser/winner pair is informative depends both on the winner and on the loser.

An antagonistic learning environment can of course always deny the learner necessary informative examples, making learning the target grammar impossible. We consider this uninteresting and assume that as long as there remain potentially informative positive examples, these are not maliciously withheld from the learner (but see chapter 5 for a discussion of the possibility of languages underdetermined by positive evidence). This still leaves a challenging problem, however. Having received a potentially informative positive example, a winner, the learner needs to find a corresponding loser that forms an informative loser/winner pair. In principle, if the winner is a parse of an input I, any of the competing parses in $Gen(I)$ can be chosen as the loser; typically, there are an infinity of choices, not all of which will lead to an informative loser/winner pair. What is needed is a procedure for choosing a loser that is guaranteed to be informative, as long as any such competitor exists.

The idea (Tesar 1998a) is simple. Consider a learner in the midst of learning, with current constraint hierarchy $\mathcal{H}$. A positive example p is received: the target parse of an input I. It is natural for the learner to compute her own parse p' for I, optimal with respect to her current hierarchy $\mathcal{H}$. If the learner's parse p' is different from the target parse p, learning should be possible; otherwise, it is not. For if the target parse p equals the learner's parse p', then p is already optimal according to $\mathcal{H}$; no demotion occurs, and no learning is possible. On the other hand, if the target parse p is not the learner's parse p', then p is suboptimal according to $\mathcal{H}$, and the hierarchy needs to be modified so that p becomes optimal. For a loser to be informative when paired with the winner p, the Harmony of the loser (according to the current $\mathcal{H}$) must be greater than the Harmony of p: only then will demotion occur to render p more harmonic than the loser. The obvious choice for this loser is p': it is of maximum Harmony according to $\mathcal{H}$, and if any competitor to the winner has higher Harmony according to $\mathcal{H}$, then p' must. The type of parsing responsible for computing p' is production-directed parsing: given an input I and a stratified hierarchy $\mathcal{H}$, compute the optimal parse(s) of I. This is the computational problem solved in a number of general cases by Tesar (1995), as discussed briefly in section 1.3.3 and more extensively in chapter 8.

If the optimal parse given the current $\mathcal{H}$, *loser*, should happen to equal the correct parse *winner*, the execution of CD will produce no change in $\mathcal{H}$: no learning can occur. In fact, CD need be executed only when there is a mismatch between the correct parse and the optimal parse assigned by the current ranking. This is an *error-driven* learning algorithm (Wexler and Culicover 1980). Each observed parse is compared with a computed parse of the input. If the two parses match, no error occurs, and so no learning takes place. If the two parses differ, the error is attributed to the current hypothesized ranking, and so CD is used to adjust the hypothesized ranking. The resulting algorithm is called *Error-Driven Constraint Demotion* (EDCD).

(3.17)   Error-Driven Constraint Demotion (EDCD) Algorithm
Given: A set *positive-data* of grammatical structural descriptions, and a constraint hierarchy ℋ*-start*.
EDCD (*positive-data*, ℋ*-start*)
ℋ := ℋ*-start*
for each description *winner* in *positive-data*
   repeat
      uf := the underlying form of *winner*
      loser := the optimal description of *uf*, using ℋ
      if (*loser* is not identical to *winner*)
         md := (*marks*(*loser*), *marks*(*winner*))
         md-canceled := Mark_Cancelation(*md*)
         ℋ*-new* := Constraint_Demotion(*md-canceled*, ℋ)
         ℋ := ℋ*-new*
      end-if
   until (*loser* is identical to *winner*)
end-for
return (ℋ)

This algorithm demonstrates that using the familiar strategy of error-driven learning does not require inviolable constraints or independently evaluable parameters. Because OT is defined by means of optimization, errors are defined with respect to the relative Harmony of several entire structural descriptions, rather than particular diagnostic criteria applied to an isolated parse. Constraint Demotion accomplishes learning precisely on the basis of the comparison of entire structural descriptions.[3]

4 Overcoming Ambiguity in Overt Forms

This chapter focuses in detail on the iterative approach to contending with hidden structure. We present simulation results, obtained by applying an iterative learning algorithm to an OT system of metrical stress grammars.

4.1 An Optimality Theoretic System of Stress Grammars

Metrical stress theory has been a domain of focus for several learning investigations. Dresher and Kaye (1990) and Dresher (1999) applied cue learning to a system of stress grammars set within the P&P framework (Chomsky 1981). Hammond (1990b) also investigated the learnability of a P&P-based analysis of stress. Approaches less closely tied to any explicit linguistic framework have also been investigated (Gupta and Touretzky 1994; Daelemans, Gillis, and Durieux 1994). Metrical stress is an appealing domain because a lot is known about it, and because it can be treated somewhat in isolation from other aspects of phonology.

Metrical stress was selected for the current investigation because it permits the issue of input/output faithfulness to be set aside. In the present analysis, underlying forms are strings of syllables, and structural descriptions assign stresses to the syllables; no insertion/deletion of syllables is considered (the learning of underlying forms is discussed in chapter 5). Thus, the underlying form for an utterance can be directly (and correctly) inferred from the overt form; the underlying form is simply the syllables of the overt form (without the stresses). The OT system given here owes much to several recent OT analyses of metrical phenomena, and captures a large set of core metrical phenomena.

Each structural description is of a single prosodic word, and all overt forms are of single prosodic words. The overt forms are strings of syllables. Each syllable of an overt form is marked as light or heavy and bears a stress level of primary, secondary, or unstressed. The overt forms range from two to seven syllables in length. A structural description is a grouping of the syllables (with their stress levels) into feet. Table 4.1 shows the pairings of overt forms and structural descriptions for the stress pattern of Garawa (Furby 1974; Hayes 1995); the analysis is taken from McCarthy and Prince 1993.

Prosodic word boundaries are denoted as square brackets, and foot boundaries are denoted as parentheses. The *Gen* function will only

Table 4.1
The Garawa stress pattern (light syllables only)

Overt Forms	Descriptions
[◡́ ◡]	[(◡́ ◡)]
[◡́ ◡ ◡]	[(◡́ ◡) ◡]
[◡́ ◡ ◡̀ ◡]	[(◡́ ◡) (◡̀ ◡)]
[◡́ ◡ ◡ ◡̀ ◡]	[(◡́ ◡) ◡ (◡̀ ◡)]
[◡́ ◡ ◡̀ ◡ ◡̀ ◡]	[(◡́ ◡) (◡̀ ◡) (◡̀ ◡)]
[◡́ ◡ ◡ ◡̀ ◡ ◡̀ ◡]	[(◡́ ◡) ◡ (◡̀ ◡) (◡̀ ◡)]

Table 4.2
The constraints

Name	Description
FootBin	Each foot must be either bimoraic or bisyllabic.
WSP	Each heavy syllable must be stressed.
Parse	Each syllable must be footed.
Main-Right	Align the head-foot with the word, right edge.
Main-Left	Align the head-foot with the word, left edge.
All-Feet-Right	Align each foot with the word, right edge.
All-Feet-Left	Align each foot with the word, left edge.
Word-Foot-Right	Align the word with some foot, right edge.
Word-Foot-Left	Align the word with some foot, left edge.
Iambic	Align each foot with its head syllable, right edge.
FootNonfinal	Each head syllable must not be final in its foot.
Nonfinal	Do not foot the final syllable of the word.

generate descriptions in which each foot has precisely one head syllable, which is the sole stress-bearing syllable of that foot. An unfooted syllable must be unstressed. *Gen* also requires that a prosodic word have precisely one head foot, whose head syllable bears main stress. If the word has any other (nonhead) feet, their head syllables each bear secondary stress. Feet are maximally bisyllabic, consisting of one or two syllables.

The system has 12 constraints, listed in table 4.2. The 12 constraints are freely rankable. The Parse constraint is violated by any unfooted syllable (Prince and Smolensky 1993; McCarthy and Prince 1993). Satisfaction of this constraint in longer forms leads to multiple feet, and thus to iterative secondary stressing. FOOTBIN (Prince and Smolensky 1993) is violated by degenerate feet (feet consisting of only a single light syllable). This constraint does not effectively constrain feet of greater than two syllables, because such feet are universally banned by *Gen* (and thus never appear in candidates). WSP, the weight-to-stress principle (Prince 1990), is violated by any heavy syllable that is unstressed.

The ALL-FEET-RIGHT/LEFT constraints pressure all feet to be as close to the right/left edge of the word as possible (McCarthy and Prince 1993). If ALL-FEET-RIGHT is undominated, optimal descriptions will have only a single foot, at the right edge of the word. When dominated by PARSE but still active, these constraints capture phenomena previously analyzed as directional iterativity. The MAIN-RIGHT/LEFT constraints are similar but only apply to the head foot of the word; they are vacuously satisfied by any feet that are not the head foot of the word. All four of these constraints are gradient alignment constraints, assessing a constraint violation for every syllable intervening between the relevant foot edge and the relevant word edge.

Two other constraints, WORD-FOOT-RIGHT/LEFT, are nongradient alignment constraints. Each requires that the relevant word edge be aligned with some foot. If the leftmost syllable of a word is not footed, a single violation of WORD-FOOT-LEFT is assessed, regardless of how far from the left edge of the word the leftmost foot is. Each of these constraints can be violated at most once in a structural description.

The system includes two foot form constraints, IAMBIC and FOOTNON-FINAL. The IAMBIC constraint requires the head syllable to be aligned with the right edge of the foot, making it final in the foot. The constraint FOOTNONFINAL (Tesar 1998c) is not the mirror image of IAMBIC, as might be expected. It not only requires that the head syllable be initial in the foot, but also that there be another syllable after it in the foot. This captures a typological asymmetry in stress systems noted by Hayes (1995): trochaic languages may be either quantity sensitive or quantity insensitive, while iambic languages are overwhelmingly quantity sensitive. The constraint was inspired by the concept of *foot extrametricality* proposed by Hammond (1990a) and discussed by Kager (1994), both of whom discussed the concept in the context of accounting for ternary systems. Our metrical system does not attempt to account for ternary systems, but adapts the idea of making the head foot nonfinal to the purpose of the foot-type asymmetry.

A sufficiently high ranking of NONFINAL produces syllable extrametricality effects (Liberman and Prince 1977; Hayes 1980). The formulation of NONFINAL given here is closer to the traditional conception of extrametricality than the formulation given in Prince and Smolensky 1993, assessing equal degree of violation to any footed final syllable, regardless of whether that syllable is stressed.

A constraint hierarchy is shown in (4.1) that generates the stress pattern for Garawa shown in table 4.1.

(4.1) {FOOTBIN FOOTNONFINAL MAIN-LEFT} ≫ PARSE ≫ ALL-FEET-RIGHT ≫ *the rest*

The three constraints in the top stratum are effectively undominated for this language: any relative ranking among them will produce the same language, so long as all three of them dominate all the remaining constraints and the other constraints are held in the same position relative to each other. High-ranked FOOTNONFINAL, in virtue of dominating IAMBIC, ensures that each foot is trochaic; a stressed syllable is aligned with the left edge of its foot. MAIN-LEFT determines that the head foot of the prosodic word (assigning main stress) is at the left edge of the word. These two constraints, ranked at the top, ensure that main stress always falls on the initial syllable. The domination of PARSE by FOOTBIN prevents degenerate feet from occurring in optimal forms. Thus, the words with an odd number of words have a single unfooted syllable. Ranking PARSE above ALL-FEET-RIGHT ensures that words with four or more syllables will have additional feet assigning secondary stresses. ALL-FEET-RIGHT dominates all the remaining constraints. It applies to each foot, and for each foot is violated by each syllable separating the foot from the right edge of the prosodic word. Obviously, at most one foot can be perfectly aligned with the right edge of the word; if there are multiple feet, some violations of the constraint are inevitable. However, the number of violations is reduced if the feet are stacked up toward the right. The effect in Garawa is seen in five- and seven-syllable words. In those words, the feet align from the right, except the head foot, which stays aligned to the left edge of the word, incurring an extra violation of ALL-FEET-RIGHT rather than a violation of higher-ranked MAIN-LEFT. Because MAIN-LEFT only applies to the head foot, it has no effect on the other feet of the word, permitting ALL-FEET-RIGHT to determine their position.

4.2   Robust Interpretive Parsing

In OT, the constraint ranking determines which of the many candidate structural descriptions is optimal (hence grammatical) for a given underlying form. This mapping provides a (highly idealized) characterization of language production as an optimization process. The process of computing the optimal structural description for an underlying form, given a constraint ranking, will be called *production-directed parsing*. The algorithms used for parsing in these simulations are based on the parsing algorithms developed by Tesar (1995, 1996). Other work on efficient algorithms for production-directed parsing with OT grammars has been done by Ellison (1994), Eisner (1997), Frank and Satta (1998), and Karttunen (1998).

A corresponding mapping for language comprehension would be one that maps from an overt form of the language to its grammatical structural description. A definition for such a mapping was suggested by Tesar and Smolensky (1998): the hearer is presented with an overt form, and selects the structural description of that overt form that is optimal with respect to their current constraint ranking. The difference is that here the candidate structural descriptions competing for optimality are candidates whose overt portions match the observed overt form. In principle, this means that structural descriptions for different underlying forms might compete with each other, if they have identical overt forms. A structural description with an overt form that matches the observed overt form is an *interpretation* of that overt form. The interpretation assigned to an overt form is the structural description that, out of all descriptions whose overt portion matches the overt form, best satisfies the ranked universal constraints. The process of computing the optimal interpretation for an overt form, given a constraint ranking, will be called *interpretive parsing*. Other work, within OT, on parsing overt forms, specifically elements of syllable structure, has been done by Hammond (1995, 1997).

Language production and language comprehension, then, are both optimization processes. When a competent speaker, possessing the correct constraint ranking, interprets an overt form, they arrive at the same structural description as when they apply production-directed processing to the corresponding underlying form. Both processes are defined in terms of optimization with respect to the same constraint ranking. What is proposed here is that a language learner uses the same processes during learning. At any given time, the learner has a ranking; this ranking is supplied to production-directed parsing when attempting to produce language, and it is supplied to interpretive parsing when the learner is interpreting the overt forms it hears (figure 4.1).

One critical property of interpretive parsing is that it is "robust" in the following sense: the process assigns a description to an overt form even when there is no description matching that overt form that is grammatical (i.e., optimal for its underlying form) according to the current ranking. A description is still assigned to the overt form, even if there is another description for the same underlying form (but with a different overt form) that better satisfies the ranked constraints. The learner can be aware that the utterance is not grammatical according to their current ranking, but nevertheless do the best they can to interpret the utterance. This reflects the observation that competent speakers can often offer consistent interpretations of utterances they simultaneously judge to be ungrammatical.

To illustrate this, consider the following example. The target language that a learner is exposed to is one with no secondary stress (i.e., main stress only), with a trochaic head foot aligned with the right edge of the prosodic word (giving penultimate main stress). However, the learner starts with a hypothesis ranking that assigns an iambic head foot aligned from the left edge of the word (giving peninitial main stress), and no secondary stress. The important part of the ranking is shown in (4.2). *Note:*

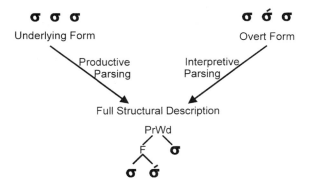

Figure 4.1
Production-directed and interpretive parsing

For spatial convenience, some constraint names will be abbreviated, such as AFL for ALL-FEET-LEFT and AFR for ALL-FEET-RIGHT.

(4.2)   AFL ≫ AFR ≫ IAMBIC ≫ MAIN-R ≫ FOOTNONFINAL ≫ *the rest*

Consider the overt form [◡ ◡ ◡ ◡́ ◡]. The learner, using the ranking in (4.2), applies interpretive parsing to arrive at the analysis of [◡ ◡ (◡ ◡́) ◡]; this is the most harmonic structural description consistent with the overt form. The learner then applies production-directed parsing to the under-lying form of five syllables, getting [(◡ ◡́) ◡ ◡ ◡]. This pair, along with their violations of the relevant constraints, is shown in table 4.3.

The optimal interpretation, [◡ ◡ (◡ ◡́) ◡], fares better on the cur-rent ranking than the other candidate consistent with the overt form, [◡ ◡ ◡ (◡́ ◡)], because it has fewer violations of ALL-FEET-LEFT. The result of production-directed parsing, [(◡ ◡́) ◡ ◡ ◡], fares better on the current ranking than the interpretive parse because it incurs fewer violations yet of ALL-FEET-LEFT (in fact, no violations at all).

From the standpoint of learning, the most important fact about these two parses is that they are not identical: the observed word was not stressed in the same way that the learner's current ranking stresses it. This mismatch causes the learner to revise their ranking hypothesis, in an effort to find a ranking that will stress the word in the same way as was observed. More precisely, the learner will use their interpretation of the surface form, [◡ ◡ (◡ ◡́) ◡], as the target, modifying the ranking in an effort to make this description the optimal one for an underlying form of five syllables.

An additional point worth noticing: the learner has misanalyzed the overt form; the correct analysis (the one assigned by the target grammar) is [◡ ◡ ◡ (◡́ ◡)]. This might be cause for concern. However, as will be

Table 4.3
The production-directed parse of five syllables better satisfies the ranked constraints than the optimal interpretation of overt form [◡ ◡ ◡ ◡́ ◡], which in turn does better than an alternative interpretation

Overt: [◡ ◡ ◡ ◡́ ◡]		AFL	AFR	IAMBIC	M-R	FTNONFINAL
Production ☞	[(◡ ◡́) ◡ ◡ ◡]		***		***	*
Interpretation ⟫	[◡ ◡ (◡ ◡́) ◡]	**	*		*	*
Alt. Interpretation	[◡ ◡ ◡ (◡́ ◡)]	***		*		

illustrated, it is possible for the learner to learn successfully even when an overt form is initially misinterpreted.

4.3 The RIP/CD Learning Procedure

To continue the example of the previous section, the learner wants to modify the ranking so that the interpretive parse, [◡ ◡ (◡ ◡́) ◡], does better than the production-directed parse. Thus, [◡ ◡ (◡ ◡́) ◡] is the winner, [(◡ ◡́) ◡ ◡ ◡] the loser. The highest-ranked constraint assessing more marks to the loser is ALL-FEET-RIGHT, so the constraint assessing more marks to the winner, ALL-FEET-LEFT, is demoted to immediately below ALL-FEET-RIGHT, into the stratum already occupied by IAMBIC; this is shown in table 4.4.

The loser now loses to the winner, because it has more violations of ALL-FEET-RIGHT. While this demotion ensures that the winner beats this loser, it does not ensure that the optimal description matches the observed overt form. Now that the learner has a new ranking, it most go back and re-parse, using the new ranking. As shown in table 4.5, the interpretation provided by interpretive parsing is now [◡ ◡ ◡ (◡́ ◡)], and the optimal description for the underlying form of five syllables is [◡ ◡ ◡ (◡ ◡́)]. Again, there is a mismatch, indicating that the learner's ranking is incorrect. Observe, however, that the best interpretation of the overt

Table 4.4
After the first demotion, the winner is more harmonic

Overt:	[◡ ◡ ◡ ◡́ ◡]	AFR	IAMBIC	AFL	MAIN-R	FTNONFINAL
Loser	[(◡ ◡́) ◡ ◡ ◡]	* * *			* * *	*
Winner	[◡ ◡ (◡ ◡́) ◡]	*		* *	*	*

Table 4.5
Loser/winner pair before the second demotion

Overt:	[◡ ◡ ◡ ◡́ ◡]	AFR	IAMBIC	AFL	MAIN-R	FTNONFINAL
Loser	[◡ ◡ ◡ (◡ ◡́)]			* * *		*
Winner	[◡ ◡ ◡ (◡́ ◡)]		*	* * *		

form now matches the structural description of the target grammar. This occurred despite the fact that the interpretation of the previous step was wrong; the algorithm used an incorrect target but nevertheless moved in the right direction.

Because of the mismatch, Constraint Demotion is now applied again, using the interpretive parse as the winner and the production-directed parse as the loser. The violations for the new winner and loser are shown in table 4.5.

The highest-ranked constraint violated more by the loser is Foot-Nonfinal. The constraint violated more by the winner, Iambic, is demoted to the stratum immediately below the one occupied by Foot-Nonfinal, the result being as depicted in table 4.6.

With the resulting ranking, both interpretive and production-oriented parsing give the same (correct) structural description. The learner has succeeded in learning a ranking generating this overt form, and in fact the target language.

A description of RIP/CD is given in (4.3). At any given time, there is a hypothesis ranking held by the learner. Given an overt form, interpretive parsing is used to determine the optimal interpretation of that overt form (under the learner's ranking). That full structural description includes an underlying form. Production-directed parsing is applied to that underlying form to obtain the structural description assigned to the underlying form by the learner's ranking. If the optimal interpretation of the overt form matches the optimal description of the underlying form, the ranking is not changed. So far as can be determined from this overt form, the learner's ranking is correct. If, on the other hand, the interpretation of the overt form given by interpretive parsing does not match the description of the underlying form generated by production-directed parsing, an error has occurred. The learner presumes the interpretive parse to be the correct analysis of the overt form and applies

Table 4.6
Loser/winner pair after the second demotion

Overt:	[˘ ˘ ˘ ´˘ ˘]		AFR	AFL	MAIN-R	FTNONFINAL	IAMBIC
Loser	[˘ ˘ ˘ (˘ ´)]			* * *		*	
Winner	[˘ ˘ ˘ (´ ˘)]			* * *			*

Constraint Demotion, with the interpretive parse as the winner and the
production-directed parse as the loser. The learner then adopts the
resulting new ranking, and the same procedure may be repeated, with
either the same overt form or other overt forms.

RIP/CD alternates structure assignment (interpretive parsing) and
grammar learning (changing the ranking), in the iterative fashion discussed in chapter 1. A hypothesis ranking is used to estimate the hidden
structure for an overt form. This hidden structure is then used to determine a new ranking. The new ranking is then used to determine a new
estimate of hidden structure, and so forth. Learning is successful if the
iterations converge: the assigned interpretations of the overt forms are
all grammatical, indicating that the ranking is consistent with the overt
forms.

(4.3)   The RIP/CD learning algorithm
Given: An overt form *overt*, and a constraint hierarchy $\mathcal{H}_0$.
RIP_CD(*overt*, $\mathcal{H}_0$)
$\mathcal{H} := \mathcal{H}_0$
repeat
   interp := interpretive_parsing(*overt*, $\mathcal{H}$)
   uf := underlying form of *interp*
   prod := production_directed_parsing(*uf*, $\mathcal{H}$)
   if (*interp* is not identical to *prod*)
     md := (*marks*(*prod*), *marks*(*interp*))
     md-canceled := Mark_Cancelation(*md*)
     $\mathcal{H}$-*new* := Constraint_Demotion(*md-canceled*, $\mathcal{H}$)
     $\mathcal{H} := \mathcal{H}$-*new*
   end-if
until (*interp* is identical to *prod*)
return ($\mathcal{H}$)

4.4   Getting Stuck: How RIP/CD Can Fail

It is unfortunate but not surprising that it is possible for this algorithm
to fail to converge on a correct ranking for a language. To date, three
kinds of failure have been observed, and they are illustrated in this
section.

4.4.1   Selecting an Interpretation That Cannot Possibly Be Optimal

As currently construed, there is no restriction on interpretive parsing to return an interpretation that is possibly optimal. If the current constraint hierarchy in use by the learner differs in the right way from the target language, it is possible for interpretive parsing to return a structural description that is not only not the structural description assigned by the target language, but is in fact a structural description that *cannot* be optimal under *any* total constraint ranking.

Nearly all the examples of this phenomenon observed in the simulations with metrical stress involved inconsistent foot form—that is, a structural description that contains both iambic and trochaic feet. Such descriptions can only occur in optimal structural descriptions under very limited circumstances. The situation usually arises when both foot form constraints, FOOTNONFINAL and IAMBIC, are near the bottom of the learner's constraint hierarchy and are dominated by most or all of the other constraints.

To illustrate, suppose that the learner's current constraint hierarchy is the one shown in (4.4) (for brevity, only certain critical constraints will be included in all the tables).

(4.4)   {FOOTBIN MAIN-L} ≫ {PARSE} ≫ {AFR} ≫ {AFL MAIN-R} ≫ {IAMBIC} ≫ {FTNONFINAL}

The learner uses robust interpretive parsing to interpret the overt form, producing an interpretation (the winner), and applies production-directed parsing to the underlying form of five light syllables, producing the currently optimal structural description (the loser). These forms are shown in table 4.7.

The only difference between the currently optimal description and the optimal interpretation is the location of stress inside the rightmost foot: the foot is iambic in the currently optimal description, and trochaic in the optimal interpretation. The bottom row of table 4.7 shows the correct structural description, the one assigned by the target language. Comparing the correct candidate to the currently optimal one reveals the key changes necessary to reach the correct ranking: MAIN-L needs to be demoted to below ALL-FEET-R, and IAMBIC needs to be demoted to below FOOTNONFINAL. However, the learner cannot see this, because they are working with the optimal interpretation.

Table 4.7
Before the first demotion: the interpretation prompts the learner to demote IAMBIC

Overt: [⏑ ⏑ ⏑ ⏑ ⏑]		PARSE	MAIN-L	AFR	IAMBIC	FTNONFINAL
currently optimal	☞ [(⏑ ⏑) ⏑ (⏑ ⏑)]	*		*** **		**
optimal interpretation	⇒ [(⏑ ⏑) ⏑ (⏑ ⏑)]	*		*** **	*	*
correct in target	✓ [⏑ (⏑ ⏑) (⏑ ⏑)]	*	*	**	**	

Table 4.8
Before the second demotion: the same interpretation prompts the learner to demote FOOTNONFINAL

Overt: [⏑ ⏑ ⏑ ⏑ ⏑]		PARSE	MAIN-L	AFR	FTNONFINAL	IAMBIC
currently optimal	☞ [(⏑ ⏑) ⏑ (⏑ ⏑)]	*		*** **		**
optimal interpretation	⇒ [(⏑ ⏑) ⏑ (⏑ ⏑)]	*		*** **	*	*
correct in target	✓ [⏑ (⏑ ⏑) (⏑ ⏑)]	*	*	**		**

Table 4.9
After the second demotion, the learner is back where they started

Overt: [⏑ ⏑ ⏑ ⏑ ⏑]		PARSE	MAIN-L	AFR	IAMBIC	FTNONFINAL
currently optimal	☞ [(⏑ ⏑) ⏑ (⏑ ⏑)]	*		*** **		**
optimal interpretation	⇒ [(⏑ ⏑) ⏑ (⏑ ⏑)]	*		*** **	*	*
correct in target	✓ [⏑ (⏑ ⏑) (⏑ ⏑)]	*	*	**	**	

The learner proceeds as usual, by identifying the constraints violated more by the optimal interpretation {IAMBIC} and demoting them below the highest constraint violated more by the currently optimal candidate {FOOTNONFINAL}. The problem is that the two candidate structural descriptions do not differ in the number of violations of MAIN-L and ALL-FEET-R: the feet are in the same place in both forms. This is because the foot form constraints are below all the relevant foot location constraints in the learner's current hierarchy, so that the learner is willing to have inconsistent foot form in order to best satisfy the foot location constraints in their interpretation of the overt form. The result of Constraint Demotion is shown in table 4.8.

The new ranking selects a new candidate as optimal: the currently optimal candidate now has two trochaic feet. However, the optimal interpretation of the overt form has not changed. This is because the selection of the optimal interpretation is still decided entirely by the dominant foot location constraints, which have not moved in the hierarchy. Unfortunately, the only difference between the new optimal description and the optimal interpretation is again the form of one foot. This time, it is the leftmost foot that the two disagree on, and the optimal interpretation has one more violation of FOOTNONFINAL, while the currently optimal description has one more violation of IAMBIC. Applying Constraint Demotion again produces the situation shown in table 4.9.

Notice that table 4.9 is identical to table 4.7, and the learner is back to the situation where this illustration began. Further application of Constraint Demotion will simply repeat the same binary pattern: demote IAMBIC below FOOTNONFINAL, then demote FOOTNONFINAL below IAMBIC, then demote IAMBIC below FOOTNONFINAL, and so on. The two foot form constraints "chase each other" at the bottom of the hierarchy, and will continue to do so until the learner gives up on the overt form.

4.4.2   The Optimal Interpretation Is Harmonically Bound

Here the interpretation returned by interpretive parsing cannot possibly be an optimal structural description under any ranking, but the resulting behavior of the learning algorithm is quite different. In this case, the interpretation not only cannot possibly be optimal, but it is in fact harmonically bound by the currently optimal description.

An example of this is shown in table 4.10. The current best interpretation has the first syllable footed by itself, preferring to violate FOOTBIN

Table 4.10
The currently optimal candidate harmonically bounds the best interpretation

Overt:	[˘ ˘ ˘ ´]		WSP	IAMBIC	PARSE	FTBIN	FTNONFIN	AFL	AFR
currently optimal	☞	[(˘ ˘) (˘ ´)]					**	**	**
optimal interpretation	⫸	[(˘) ˘ (˘ ´)]			*	*	**	**	***
correct in target	✓	[(˘ ˘) (˘ ´)]		*			*	**	**

Table 4.11
The learner's wrong interpretation is possibly optimal

Overt:	[˘ ´ ˘]		WSP	FTBIN	MAINL	FTNONFIN	PARSE	WFR	NONFIN
currently optimal	☞	[(˘ ´) (˘ ˘)]							*
optimal interpretation	⫸	[(˘ ´) ˘ ˘]				*	**	*	
correct in target	✓	[˘ (˘ ´) ˘]			*	**	**		

Table 4.12
The learner returns to the first ranking

Overt:	[˘ ˘ ˘ ˘]		WSP	FTBIN	MAINL	FNF	NONFIN	PARSE	WFR
currently optimal	☞	[(´ ˘) ˘ ˘]						**	*
optimal interpretation	⫸	[(´ ˘) (˘ ˘)]					*		
correct in target	✓	[(´ ˘) (˘ ˘)]					*		

in deference to the higher-ranked IAMBIC. This description is harmonically bound by the currently optimal structural description (the one returned by production-directed parsing): the best interpretation has violations of PARSE, FOOTBIN, and one more violation of AFR. There are no constraints that assess more violations to the currently optimal form than to the best interpretation. Thus, Constraint Demotion can identify three constraints to demote but cannot determine what to demote them below: there are no uncanceled loser marks. Notice that if the learner were to somehow obtain the correct structural description, Constraint Demotion would succeed as expected, by demoting IAMBIC to below FOOTNONFINAL.

Because there are no uncanceled marks assessed to the currently optimal description (the loser), Constraint Demotion is stopped dead in its tracks. The silver lining is the learner knows immediately that the current best interpretation cannot be the correct structural description in the target language. In the simulations, when such a state was reached, the learner immediately abandoned the overt form, in the hopes that its constraint hierarchy would be sufficiently improved on the basis of other forms before it encountered this overt form again.

4.4.3   Endless Alternation between Different Overt Forms

In this situation, the learner can converge to an optimal grammar for any one overt form, but the grammar selected for one always fails for some other overt form, and vice versa. A specific case is shown in table 4.11.

The incorrect analysis results from the unfortunate high ranking of MAINLEFT above FOOTNONFINAL. In the target language, the head foot is in fact aligned with the left edge of the word, consistent with a high ranking of MAINLEFT, *except* when this would conflict with WSP and FTBIN. This conflict can only happen when the second syllable is heavy and the first syllable is light. The incorrect placement of the head foot by itself would not be enough to tip off the learner that anything was amiss; if the overt form only had main stress on the second syllable, the learner would be unable to detect the error. However, the misalignment of the head foot makes room, in the form of two light syllables, for a second binary foot, which then adds a secondary stress not present in the observed overt form.

Note that, while the interpretation arrived at via robust interpretive parsing is incorrect for the target language, it is nevertheless a possible optimal description (it is in fact optimal in some other languages). Thus, when the learner demotes PARSE and WORD-FOOT-RIGHT to below NON-FINAL, the result is apparent success, because the learner's interpretation is in fact optimal for the new ranking.

The learner then proceeds to other forms, unaware of any problem, until the other crucial piece of data is encountered (table 4.12).

To add insult to injury, the learner in fact has the correct interpretation of the overt form here. However, this analysis alone is not sufficient to get the learner all the way to the correct ranking. The learner, in response to this error, demotes NONFINAL to below PARSE and WORD-FOOTRIGHT. That simply puts the learner right back where they were at the beginning of this example. The learner has undone the damage of the previous misanalysis, but that only sets them up to make the same misanalysis the next time the previous form is encountered.

4.5   Simulation Results: Metrical Stress

The simulations used the overt forms of 124 of the languages generatable by the OT system. This is nowhere near the complete set of languages realizable by the system, but the 124 languages included most of the familiar metrical phenomena analyzable by this system.

Each language was presented to the learner as a set of 62 overt forms. The 62 overt forms for each language were taken from the optimal structural descriptions for all possible underlying forms of length two through five syllables (all possible combinations of light and heavy syllables), plus underlying forms of six and seven light syllables. The learning algorithm processed the forms in order by length, shortest to longest, starting over at the beginning of the list once the end was reached. The algorithm was judged to have successfully learned a language when it made a complete pass through all the forms without a single error (all the overt forms were parsed as grammatical). The learning algorithm was declared to have failed on a language when it made five passes through the overt forms without success.

When processing each overt form, robust interpretive parsing and production-directed parsing were applied to check for an error. If an error was detected, the constraint ranking was modified via Constraint Demotion as specified by the algorithm. Each such performance of Constraint Demotion was counted as a learning step, for purposes of measuring performance. Up to five learning steps were permitted in the processing of an overt form at one time. If the overt form still was giving an error after five steps, the algorithm abandoned the overt form (for that time around) and reset the constraint hierarchy to what it was before it began processing that form. The five learning steps performed were still included in the overall count for that language, however.

Three different initial constraint hierarchies were tried, and separate results are reported for each initial hierarchy.

4.5.1 Monostratal Initial Hierarchy

The monostratal hierarchy has all the constraints in a single stratum.

(4.5) {WSP FtNonfinal Iambic Parse FootBin WFL WFR Main-L Main-R AFL AFR Nonfinal}

The results are summarized in table 4.13.

There are a significant number of failures. However, when the algorithm converges, it usually does so rapidly; the number of learning steps is usually less than the number of constraints.

4.5.2 Foot Form Constraints over the Rest

The second initial hierarchy has two strata: the first stratum contains the two foot form constraints, and the second stratum contains the rest of the constraints.

(4.6) {FtNonfinal Iambic} ≫ {the rest}

The intuition behind this is to avoid the problem of the foot form constraints both ending up too low in the hierarchy by starting them above the other constraints (table 4.14).

The number of learned hierarchies has improved over the monostratal initial hierarchy case. The performance has also improved, with the median number of steps dropping from 8 to 6.

Table 4.13
Simulation results, monostratal initial hierarchy

Number of Languages	Number of Successes	Number of Failures	Number of Learning Steps	
			Median	Range
124	75	49	8	3 .. 60

Table 4.14
Simulation results, foot form constraints over the rest initial hierarchy

Number of	Number of	Number of	Number of Learning Steps	
Languages	Successes	Failures	Median	Range
124	94	30	6	2 .. 14

Table 4.15
Simulation results, WSP over foot form over the rest initial hierarchy

Number of	Number of	Number of	Number of Learning Steps	
Languages	Successes	Failures	Median	Range
124	120	4	7	2 .. 14

4.5.3 WSP over Foot Form over the Rest

The third initial hierarchy was similar to the second, but with WSP placed in a top hierarchy over the foot form constraints.

(4.7)   {WSP} ≫ {FTNONFINAL IAMBIC} ≫ {*the rest*}

This case started out with WSP at the top. If the language was strongly quantity sensitive, WSP would likely stay there. If the language required one of the foot form constraints to dominate WSP, then the WSP would be demoted to below the foot form constraints. The intuition is that either way, the interaction between the foot form constraints and WSP should not often require a demotion of both foot form constraints (table 4.15).

In this case, nearly all the languages are successfully learned. The performance is comparable to the previous case, with the majority of languages being learned in fewer learning steps than the number of constraints.

4.6 Discussion

4.6.1 Possible Future Work

To put these simulation results in perspective, it is helpful to recall some details of the specific problem being attacked. The system has 12 constraints, so there are 12! = 479,001,600 different total rankings of the constraints. The number of stratified hierarchies is several times larger yet. That is the hypothesis space that the algorithm successfully navigates in an average of about 7 steps (a step count well below the number of constraints). When the algorithm succeeds, it does so extremely quickly.

This speed makes it possible to consider several strategies for contending with convergence failure, including strategies not further explored here. Aficionados of random search algorithms might wish to consider putting a time limit on the number of learning steps allotted to a given starting hierarchy. If the algorithm has not converged to successful constraint hierarchy within, say, 20 steps, randomly select a new starting hierarchy, and continue from there with the subsequent data. Such an approach could afford many, many restarts before the number of learning steps reached the number of steps used in a typical run of many other random search algorithms on comparably sized spaces.

The effects of specific starting hierarchies might suggest an alternative to randomly selecting starting hierarchies. An analysis of a particular system might reveal a small set of starting hierarchies, such that every possible language can be learned when starting from at least one of them. The learner could then try each of them in turn until a correct hierarchy is reached, using a step count limit to decide when to abandon one hypothesis in favor of the next initial hierarchy. The price to be paid for this, of course, is the reliance on details of specific analyses; such an approach would no longer automatically generalize to all OT analyses (this is a step in the direction of cue learning).

The observed ways in which RIP/CD failed probably hold the larger significance for the possibility of any future strong formal results. The vast majority of failures in the simulations were cases where robust interpretive parsing returned (as the optimal interpretation) a structural description that was not possibly optimal. This fact invites one to search for a way to constrain robust interpretive parsing so that it can only return structural descriptions that are possibly optimal. Such an effort has its challenges. First, it simply is not obvious how to implement the constraint. A pessimist might legitimately fear that, in the general case, determining if a given structural description is possibly optimal requires applying a full learning procedure to search for a constraint hierarchy making that description optimal. Second, modifying robust interpretive parsing toward this goal might inflate the maximally austere parsing requirements of the current algorithm. The learning algorithm presented in this book requires nothing of the parsing algorithms beyond what is already required by the demands of normal language processing. Restricting robust interpretive parsing to only return possibly optimal structural descriptions might require additional parsing machinery, machinery that is not strictly necessary for normal language processing. Specific proposals along these lines will have to be examined in order to determine if the benefits justify the price.

4.6.2   What Has Been Accomplished

The simulation results for RIP/CD demonstrate several things. It is possible to make significant headway on the problem of learning hidden structure without assuming that the learner must completely, correctly learn the grammar prior to assigning hidden structure, or vice versa. The learning algorithm adapts, for OT, the iterative strategy that has been employed in statistical learning contexts, and it does so without having to give up any of the benefits of a strong linguistic theory. Straight statistical approaches to language learning (e.g., those employing hidden Markov models and stochastic context-free grammars) typically use parametrically uniform and linguistically uninformed grammar hypothesis spaces. In contrast, RIP/CD preserves the full typological restrictions of OT; the possible systems learnable by RIP/CD are the possible constraint rankings of the OT system in use. The combination of iterative-style learning and strong linguistic prediction does not come for free; the success relies crucially on the fact that OT successfully defines grammaticality in terms of optimization relative to strictly ranked, violable constraints.

The commitment to the central principles of OT does not, however, limit RIP/CD to specific linguistic phenomena; it can be applied to any linguistic domain admitting an OT analysis. In particular, the core elements of the learning theory do not require detailed knowledge and analysis of the domain-specific details of a particular account. RIP/CD requires only those constructs that must be present independent of any learning concerns. There must be a capacity for realizing structural descriptions and their constraint violations, there must be a hierarchy of violable constraints, and there must be basic language processing mechanisms informed by *Gen* and the constraint hierarchy.

RIP/CD does not require any separate catalog of the overt consequences of particular interactions between particular constraints. It contrasts rather strongly in this regard with the cue learning approach. The specification of a cue for a parameter must be done with the full knowledge of the overt consequences of that parameter setting. Not only must the cue specification contain descriptions of specific overt configurations, but it requires an analysis of the consequences of different parameter settings. For RIP/CD, the only possible role of interaction preanalysis is in the determination of an initial hierarchy (a construct necessary anyway). RIP/CD encapsulates knowledge of the substantive content of the constraints and the consequences of constraint interaction for specific forms within the language processing mechanisms. Parsing, both production-directed and interpretive, mediates between the specifics of the data (overt forms and structural descriptions) and constraint violations (just as it does in normal language use, independent of learning). This allows the learning theory to be defined over the constraint violations assessed to candidates, structures general to OT and independent of any particular linguistic domain.

The simulation results show that relinquishing preanalysis does not necessarily doom a learner to large data requirements proportionate with the space of possible grammars. RIP/CD's convergence time, measured in demotion steps, is not only far less than the number of distinct total rankings, but in most cases is below the actual number of constraints itself (a median of 7 demotion steps, for a system with 12 constraints). This speed of convergence contrasts greatly with that of general search procedures over parametric spaces, such as the triggering learning algorithm (TLA). The TLA employs a linguistically informed hypothesis space and encapsulates the substantive consequences of constraints within a parsing mechanism. However, the encapsulation is so severe that the only information provided to the learner is a success/error signal. An error signal tells the learner that their current parameter settings are collectively incorrect, without providing any information at all about which parameters require changing. The result is a random search, with convergence times growing with the size of the hypothesis space (which itself grows exponentially).

RIP/CD escapes the fate of TLA because the encapsulation of substantive linguistic information within the processing mechanisms lets more information through to the learner than just success/error. For RIP/CD, an error is accompanied by a competing candidate (the loser) with specified constraint violations. Comparing the winner's constraint violations with those of the loser provides an indication to the learner of how to change the grammar. This indication need not be perfect in order to be useful. As shown in the example of section 4.3, an initial misanalysis by robust interpretive parsing can still be informative, due to the fact that it is still constrained to match the overt form.

The example of section 4.3 also highlights another distinction between RIP/CD and the TLA: RIP/CD does not need to reach a grammar capable of analyzing the overt form in a single step. In that example, a grammar consistent with the overt form was reached after two demotion steps. RIP/CD does not need to give up on an overt form after one learning step, because it has reason to believe that the one step is progress, and that further steps would result in further progress toward the analysis of the overt form. For the TLA, if one step (the change of one parameter) fails to permit the successful parse of the overt form, it has no basis for believing that the parameter change is any kind of improvement whatsoever. The all-or-nothing character of the information provided by parsing to the TLA means that the TLA cannot have a notion of "making progress" toward an overt form. Either the TLA reaches a grammar consistent with the overt form in one step, or it stays in place. Because RIP/CD can effectively take more than one learning step in response to an overt form, it can take strong advantage of overt forms whose consistent grammars are more than one learning step away from its current hypothesis. This renders useful, to RIP/CD, a wide range of data that is not useful to the TLA, analogically speaking.

RIP/CD strikes a balance, allowing linguistically informed learning without encoding comprehensive structural detail within the learning principles. By relying on the processing mechanisms to provide constraint violations for the winner and the loser, the learner has access to information powerful enough to direct learning without being so specific as to tie the learning algorithm to a particular linguistic domain.

5 Issues in Language Learning

5.1 The Subset Principle, Richness of the Base, and Acquisition Theory

The results of chapter 3 demonstrate that our grammar learning problem is efficiently solvable by EDCD. These results apply regardless of the initial hierarchy used, and thus do not tell us anything about the initial state. As pointed out to us by Alan Prince (personal communication, 1993), however, some progress can be made, if we turn to the principle of richness of the base, repeated here in (5.1).

(5.1) *Richness of the base:* The set of possible inputs to the grammars of all languages is the same. The grammatical inventories of languages are defined as the forms appearing in the outputs that emerge from the grammar when it is fed the universal set of all possible inputs.

Richness of the base has significant implications for the explanatory role of the grammar, in particular the relationship between the *faithfulness* constraints (e.g., PARSE and FILL) and the *structural* constraints. Recall that the faithfulness constraints require the overt structure of a description to match the underlying form. For marked structures to appear in overt structures, one or more of the faithfulness constraints must dominate the structural constraints violated by the marked structure. Conversely, a language in which a marked structure never appears is properly explained by having the relevant structural constraints dominate the faithfulness constraints.

Consider CVT. A language like L_1, all of whose lexical items surface as sequences of .CV. syllables, has a systematic property. This cannot be explained by stipulating special structure in the lexicon, namely, a lexicon of underlying forms consisting only of CV sequences. It is not sufficient that the grammar yield .CV. outputs when given only CV inputs: it must give .CV. outputs even when the input is, say, /VCVC/, as shown in table 2.1. This can only be achieved by rankings in which faithfulness constraints are dominated by the structural constraints. The ranking in (2.11) provides an example.

What kind of evidence could lead the learner to select the correct hierarchy? One possibility is grammatical alternations. Alternations occur precisely because the underlying form of an item is altered in some environments in order to satisfy high-ranked structural constraints, at the expense of faithfulness. When learning the underlying forms, the learner could use the alternations as evidence that faithfulness constraints are dominated.

But what about cases in which evidence from alternation is absent? Prince suggests that perhaps the *initial hierarchy* has the faithfulness constraints lower ranked than the structural constraints. The idea is that structural constraints will only be demoted below the faithfulness constraints in response to the appearance of marked forms in observed overt structures. This proposal is similar in spirit to the Subset Principle (Angluin 1978, Berwick 1986, Pinker 1986, Wexler and Manzini 1987). Because .CV. syllables are unmarked—that is, they violate no syllable structure constraints—all languages include them in their syllable structure inventory; other, marked, syllable structures may or may not appear in the inventory. Starting with the faithfulness constraints below the syllable structure constraints means starting with the smallest syllable inventory: only the unmarked syllable. If positive evidence is presented showing that marked syllables must also be allowed, the constraint violations of the marked syllables will force demotions of structural constraints below faithfulness so that underlying structures like /CVC/ can surface as .CVC. But if no positive evidence is provided for admitting marked syllables into the inventory, the initial, smallest, inventory will remain.

One notable advantage of the latter proposal is that it accords well with recent work in child phonological acquisition (Pater and Paradis 1996, Demuth 1995, Gnanadesikan 1995, Levelt 1995; for a different view, see Hale and Reiss 1998). This work has argued that a range of empirical generalizations concerning phonological acquisition can be modeled by constraint reranking. This work proceeds from two assumptions.

(5.2)   Assumptions of OT acquisition work
a. The child's input is close to the adult form.
b. The initial ranking is one in which the faithfulness constraints are dominated by the structural constraints.

We have just sketched an argument that learnability of languages with unmarked inventories requires that (5.2b) hold (for a more complete version of this argument, see Smolensky 1996b). Assumption (5.2a) too can be explained using ideas developed here. It can also be shown (Smolensky 1996a) that robust interpretive parsing explains how the child's lexical entries can be quite "faithful" to adult forms even when their grammars, characterized by property (5.2b), produce outputs that are massively "unfaithful" to the adult forms (and to the child's inputs). Thus the learnability considerations of this book have significant implications for the foundations of current OT work in child language.

5.2 Learning Underlying Forms

According to the principle of richness of the base, the set of possible underlying forms is universal; since we are assuming here that knowledge of universals need not be learned, in a sense there is no learning problem for possible underlying forms. For interesting aspects of syntax, this is pretty much all that need be said. In OT analyses of grammatical voice systems (Legendre, Raymond, and Smolensky 1993), inversion (Grimshaw 1993, 1997), wh-questions (Billings and Rudin 1994; Legendre et al. 1995; Ackema and Neeleman 1998; Legendre, Smolensky, and Wilson 1998), and null subjects (Grimshaw and Samek-Lodovici 1995; Samek-Lodovici 1996), the set of underlying forms is universal, and all crosslinguistic variation arises from the grammar: the constraint ranking is all that need be learned. The inputs in these syntactic analyses are all some kind of predicate/argument structure, the kind of semantic structure that has often been taken as available to the syntactic learner independently of the overt data (e.g., Hamburger and Wexler 1973).

In phonology, however, there is usually an additional layer to the question of the underlying forms. While it is as true of phonology as of syntax that richness of the base entails a universal input set, there is the further question of which of the universally available inputs is paired with particular morphemes: the problem of learning the language-dependent underlying forms of morphemes.[1]

This problem was addressed in P&S chapter 9, where the following principle was developed:

(5.3) Lexicon optimization
Suppose we are given an overt structure φ and a grammar. Consider all structural descriptions (of all inputs) with overt part equal to φ; let the one with maximal Harmony be p, a parse of some input I. Then I is assigned as the underlying form of φ.[2]

For the moment, we retain the original context of this principle, and assume the correct grammar has already been learned; lexicon optimization is then used to acquire new lexical entries.

We take this principle as our starting point, and extend it to cope with phonological alternations. Consider the alternations due to syllable-final devoicing in German, illustrated in (5.4).

(5.4)   German syllable-final devoicing
a. [tak] "day" nom sing
b. [tag + ə] "days" nom pl

Presented with (5.4a) only, lexicon optimization chooses /tak/ as the underlying form of "day"; assuming the correct (devoicing) grammar, there are two underlying forms to choose from: /tak/ and /tag/. Both surface as [tak], but /tag/ does so with additional marks: FAITHFULNESS violations (the voicing feature in the final underlying segment of /tag/ is not realized in the surface form [tak]). The less marked structural description thus arises from the underlying form /tak/, which is therefore selected by lexicon optimization. In general, lexicon optimization (in its simplest form) minimizes deep/surface disparities in its selection of underlying forms.

But if presented with (5.4b) only, minimizing deep/surface disparities will lead lexicon optimization to choose /tag/ for "day". Thus in its bare formulation, this principle is indeterminate in the face of alternations. As this example clearly shows, we really need to apply lexicon optimization not to individual forms, but to entire *paradigms*.[3]

This conclusion converges with several lines of research in OT phonology that, independently of any learning considerations, point to the conclusion that, in general, grammatical optimization needs to be performed at the level of the paradigm. In a variety of contexts (e.g., "cyclic effects"), phonological explanation seems to require identity of the expression of a morpheme across its paradigm: what Burzio (1993, 1994, 1995, 1998, to appear) has termed *antiallomorphy*, or in other terms, *Faithfulness* constraints holding between pairs of outputs in the same paradigm (Benua 1995; Buckley 1995; Flemming and Kenstowicz 1995; Kenstowicz 1995a, 1995b; McCarthy 1995; Gafos 1996). We will call such constraints OO-FAITH for "output/output faithfulness".

Interestingly, paradigm-level optimization in phonology proper is typically needed in cases where expected alternation does not occur (antial-

Table 5.1
Paradigm tableau with phonological alternation

/tag/ + {Ø, ə}		*overt part*	ONSFAITH	*VOI	FAITH	OO-FAITH
(a) ☞	{ .tag$_{<voi>}$. / .ta.g+ə. }	{ [tak] / [tagə] }		. *	*	*
(b)	{ .tag. / .ta.g+ə. }	{ [tag] / [tagə] }		* *		
(c)	{ .tag$_{<voi>}$. / .tag$_{<voi>}$+ə. }	{ [tak] / [takə] }	*		* *	

lomorphy); paradigm-level *lexicon* optimization is needed in cases when alternation *does* occur. In (5.4), for example, OO-FAITH constraints demanding identity of expression of German "day" in different environments must be outranked by the constraints that enforce syllable-final devoicing. Adopting the analysis of syllable-final devoicing of Lombardi (1995), we have the miniature *paradigm tableau* in table 5.1. ONSFAITH requires faithfulness in onset segments; this positionally sensitive faithfulness constraint is the key to Lombardi's analysis of coda devoicing: *VOI prohibits voicing generally, but this is overridden in the onset by faithfulness to underlying voicing.

This tableau shows how the choice of underlying form /tag/ is parsed by the correct (devoicing) grammar, in the part of its paradigm corresponding to nominative singular and plural. Three candidate paradigm fragments are shown. In the first candidate paradigm, (a), in the singular, the voicing feature of the final /g/ is unparsed (thus unrealized): the surface form is [tak]; in the plural, this feature is parsed. This candidate paradigm violates three constraints: *VOI, which prohibits voicing; general faithfulness constraints denoted "FAITH", in virtue of failing to parse the underlying feature; and the OO-FAITH constraint, since the expression of "day" differs in singular and plural. Despite these three violations, (a) is the optimal candidate paradigm. Candidate paradigms (b) and (c) both obey OO-FAITH: in (b), "day" surfaces as [tag] in both singular and plural, while in (c), it surfaces uniformly as [tak]. However, (b) loses to (a) because (a) better satisfies *VOI; (c) loses to (a) because (c) violates top-ranked ONSFAITH.[4]

Our interest in paradigm optimization here concerns the acquisition of underlying forms. We propose to apply lexicon optimization at the paradigm level: the underlying form of a morpheme is the one, among all those that give the correct surface forms, that yields the maximum-Harmony paradigm (table 5.2).

In this lexicon optimization tableau,[5] we compare two underlying forms for "day", /tag/ and /tak/, both parsed so that they surface with the correct surface form paradigm, {[tak], [tagə]}. In the first candidate paradigm, the alternation is achieved by underparsing an underlying voice feature of the final /g/, while in the second candidate paradigm, alternation occurs through *over*parsing: *Gen* has added a voice feature to the underlying /k/. In the second candidate, the unfaithful parsing occurs in onset position, while in the first candidate paradigm it appears in coda position. Thus in addition to the constraint violations of the first candidate paradigm, the second candidate paradigm incurs a violation of ONSFAITH: (b) is thus less harmonic than (a). Lexicon optimization picks /tag/ as the underlying form because it gives rise to the most harmonic structural description of the paradigm.

So far, we have assumed that the correct grammar has already been learned. In reality, of course, underlying forms and grammars must be learned simultaneously, to a considerable extent. In the case of phonology, the interpretive parser required in the RIP/CD algorithm for acquiring the grammar must have access to the lexicon of underlying forms[6]: the parser must know, for example, that the correct interpretive parse of [tak] is .tag$_{\langle voi \rangle}$. and not .tak., because the underlying form is /tag/ and not /tak/.

This adds one additional dimension of complexity to the full iterative algorithm ultimately needed to acquire phonology. *Three* components must now function in concert:

• A robust parser that adds hidden structures to overt learning data, assuming the current grammar and lexicon of underlying forms (the RIP component).

• A grammar learner, which reranks constraints to make optimal the structural descriptions generated by the parser (the CD component).

• A lexicon learner, which takes the current grammar and overt learning data and derives underlying forms.

For the last component, we propose lexicon optimization, operating at the level of the morphological paradigm (the "paradigmatic lexicon

Table 5.2
Lexicon optimization tableau for [tak] ~ [tagə]

			overt part	OnsFaith	*Voi	Faith	OO-Faith
(a) ☞	/tag/ + {Ø/ə}	→	{.tag$_{<voi>}$. / .ta.g+ə.} {[tak] / [tagə]}		*	*	*
(b)	/tak/ + {Ø/ə}	→	{.tak. / .ta.k$_{[voi]}$+ə.} {[tak] / [tagə]}	*	*	*	*

Table 5.3
Three directions of Harmony optimization

	Type of Optimization	Given…	Compute…	Examples	
(a)	Production-Directed Parsing	/I/	.p., [φ]	/tag/ →	.tag$_{(voi)}$., [tak]
(b)	Paradigmatic Lexicon Optimization	{[φ]}	{.p.}, {/I/}	{[tak] / [tagə]} →	{.tag$_{(voi)}$., /tag/ / .ta.g+ə. /ə-/ , /ə-/ }
(c)	Robust Interpretive Parsing	[φ], {/I/}	.p.	[tak],{/tag/,....} →	.tag$_{(voi)}$.
				[tagə],{/tag/,....} →	.ta.g+ə.

/I/ = underlying form

.p. = structural description

[φ] = overt form (with morphological structure)

{/I/} = lexicon of underlying forms

{.p.} = paradigm of structural descriptions

{[φ]} = paradigm of overt forms

optimization" or "PLO" component). As described in section 1.3, the overall strategy deriving from iterative model-based learning algorithms is to design components that correctly compute their answers, assuming the other components have correctly computed their answers—and then to show that, starting from an initial guess, the components iteratively converge to a correct state (figure 5.1). This is one of the next steps in the research program developed here: study of the three-component RIP/CD/PLO algorithm.[7]

The components of the learning system we have proposed are all strongly shaped by the optimization character of the grammar being acquired. Lexicon optimization, robust interpretive parsing, and the optimization usually taken to define the operation of an OT grammar, production-directed parsing, are all merely different ways of accessing the evaluative structure that is an OT grammar. An OT grammar assigns a Harmony value to a structural description or parse p that includes an input I and an overt part φ. As shown in table 5.3, we have exploited three different ways of maximizing Harmony.

In its usual operation, the OT grammar takes an input I and produces as output the structure p (including overt part φ) that has maximal Harmony, among all structures that parse the given input I. This is shown

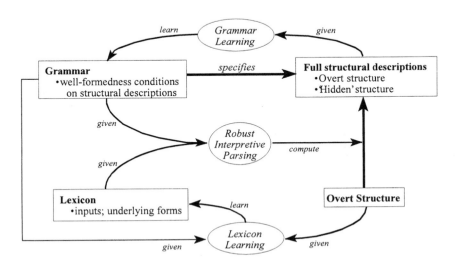

Figure 5.1
Problem decomposition, including the lexicon

in row (a) of table 5.3. For example, given an input /tag/, in the grammar of table 5.1, .tag$_{\langle voi \rangle}$. (overt: [tak]) is the structural description with greater Harmony than any other parse of /tag/.

In paradigmatic lexicon optimization, we start with a surface form φ, finding the complete structural description *p* that maximizes Harmony, among all structural descriptions with overt part φ. This was just illustrated for the example shown in row (b) of table 5.3.

Robust interpretive parsing is yet a third direction in which to perform optimization. Given an overt form φ, we find the structural description with overt part φ that has maximal Harmony, considering only inputs found in the given lexicon {/*I*/}. The example shown in row (c) of table 5.3 was mentioned a few paragraphs earlier: assuming a grammar for German, the interpretive parse that has maximal Harmony among all those with the given phonetic form [tak] is of course .tak.; but restricting to underlying forms in the German lexicon, which lacks /tak/, the maximal Harmony form is .tag$_{\langle voi \rangle}$., with underlying form /tag/.

Thus we see that the particular structure of grammar under OT—optimization relative to a hierarchy of constraints—enables us to intimately tie learning the lexicon of underlying forms to the basic operation of the grammar—pairing output structures to inputs—as well as to the assignment of hidden structure to overt learning data. All three are simply different ways of deploying the core function of the grammar: assessing the Harmony of structural descriptions.

6 Learnability and Linguistic Theory

6.1 Parametric Independence and Linguistic Explanation

Let us consider an important learnability consequence of the different conceptions of crosslinguistic variation found in OT and in the P&P framework. In P&P theory, crosslinguistic variation is accounted for by a set of parameters, where a specific grammar is determined by fixing each parameter to one of its possible values. Work on learnability focuses on the relationship between data and the parameter values, usually discussed in terms of triggers. A *trigger* is a datum (e.g., for syntax, a type of sentence) that indicates the appropriate value for a specific parameter (see, for example, the definitions of trigger in Gibson and Wexler 1994, Frank and Kapur 1996). It is significant that a trigger provides information about the value of a single parameter, rather than relationships between the values of several parameters.[1] This property is further reinforced by a proposed constraint on learning, the Single Value Constraint (Clark 1990, Gibson and Wexler 1994): successive hypotheses considered by a learner may differ by the value of at most one parameter. The result is that learnability concerns in the P&P framework favor parameters that are independent: they interact with each other as little as possible, so that the effects of each parameter setting can be distinguished from the effects of the other parameters. In fact, this property of independence has been proposed as a principle for grammars (Wexler and Manzini 1987). Unfortunately, this results in a conflict between the goals of learnability, which favor independent parameters with restricted effects, and the goals of linguistic theory, which favor parameters with wide-ranging effects and greater explanatory power (see Safir 1987 for a discussion of this conflict).

OT may provide the opportunity for this conflict to be avoided. In OT, interaction between constraints is not only possible but explanatorily crucial. Crosslinguistic variation is explained not by variation in the substance of individual constraints, but by variation in the relative ranking of the same constraints. Crosslinguistic variation is thus only possible to the extent that constraints interact. The Constraint Demotion learning algorithm not only tolerates constraint interaction, but is based entirely on it. Informative data provide information not about one constraint in isolation, but about the results of interaction between constraints. Constraints that have wide-ranging effects benefit learnability. Thus the results presented here provide evidence that in OT, linguistic explanation and learnability work together: they both favor interacting constraints with wide-ranging effects and explanatory power.

This attractive feature arises from the fact that OT defines grammaticality in terms of optimization over violable constraints. This central principle makes constraint interaction the main explanatory mechanism. It provides the implicit negative data used by Constraint Demotion precisely because it defines grammaticality in terms of the comparison of candidate descriptions, rather than in terms of the structure of each candidate description in isolation. Constraint Demotion proceeds by comparing the constraint violations incurred by candidate structural descriptions. This makes constraint interaction the basis for learning.

By making constraint interaction the foundation of both linguistic explanation and learning, OT creates the opportunity for the full alignment of these two goals. The discovery of sets of constraints that interact strongly in ways that participate in diverse linguistic phenomena represents progress for both theoretical explanation and learnability. Clearly, this is a desirable property for a theoretical framework.

6.2 Summary

An OT grammar is a ranked set of violable constraints that defines a notion of relative Harmony of structural descriptions, the maximally harmonic or optimal structures being the grammatical ones. The consequences of constraint hierarchies for surface patterns can be quite subtle and often surprising. Remarkably different surface patterns can emerge from the reranking of the same set of universal constraints.

All this is integral to the explanatory power of OT as a linguistic theory. But it also raises concerns about learnability. If the relations between grammatical forms and grammars are so complex and opaque, how can a child cope?

Linguists working in OT are frequently faced with a hypothesized set of universal constraints and a collection of surface forms to which they have given hypothetical structural descriptions; the question is, is there a ranking of the constraints that yields the correct structures? Typically, this turns out to be a challenging question to answer. Of course, with even a modest number of constraints, the number of possible rankings is much too large to explore exhaustively.

So the starting point of the present research is this question: Are there reliable, efficient means for finding a ranking of a given set of constraints that correctly yields a given set of grammatical structural descriptions? The answer is yes, if the learner is given informative pairs of optimal structures with suboptimal competitors. For any set of such data pairs consistent with some unknown total ranking of the given constraints, Constraint Demotion finds a stratified hierarchy consistent with all the data pairs.

A key to these results is the implicit negative evidence that comes with each positive example: all the universally given competitors to each optimal structure (excluding any that may have identical constraint violations); these are guaranteed to be suboptimal and therefore ill formed. The pairs of optimal forms and suboptimal competitors are the basis of Constraint Demotion: the constraints violated by the optimal form are minimally demoted to lie below some constraint violated by the suboptimal form (excluding canceled marks).

Is it necessary that informative suboptimal forms be provided to the learner? The answer is no. Given a grammatical structural description as a learning datum, the learner can identify the input in the structural description, and compute the optimal parse of that input using the currently hypothesized hierarchy. That parse can be used as the suboptimal competitor, unless it is equal to the given parse, in which case the example is not informative—no learning can occur. This is EDCD.

In the cases mentioned so far, the learning procedure can be proved to converge to a correct hierarchy, as shown in chapter 7. These results all assume that learning begins with no relative ranking of constraints: all constraints begin at the top of the hierarchy, and some are then demoted. Does learnability depend on this assumption about the initial state? The answer is no; the same results can be shown to follow when the initial state is any arbitrary hierarchy.

Learning in all these cases is efficient, in the sense that the number of informative examples, or number of learning operations (demotions), is guaranteed to be no more than $N(N-1)$, where N is the number of constraints. This grows quite modestly with N, and is vastly less than the number of grammars, $N!$.

Must full structural descriptions of positive examples be provided to the learner? The answer is no; the learner, given only the overt part of grammatical structures, can compute the full structural descriptions needed for Constraint Demotion by using robust interpretive parsing. Using the currently hypothesized grammar, the learner finds the maximal-Harmony structural description consistent with the overt form (and the currently hypothesized lexicon). Such parsing is a necessary part of the overall theory anyway, independent of learning, since grammar users must perform it when interpreting overt forms. Coupling interpretive parsing to the Constraint Demotion solution to the problem of learning a grammar from full structural descriptions yields an algorithm, RIP/CD, a new member of the family of iterative model-based solutions to the general problem of learning hidden structure. The results of the computer experiments suggest that RIP/CD is a viable approach, and in particular that the formal data complexity results for constraint demotion do in fact carry over into the performance of full RIP/CD.

In the case of phonology acquisition, must the learner be provided with the lexicon of underlying forms (necessary for interpretive parsing, as well as the inputs to production-directed grammatical parsing)? We propose that, as part of the same iterative process that is adapting the grammar to accommodate the structural descriptions produced by interpretive parsing (RIP/CD), the learner can incrementally learn the lexicon via lexicon optimization at the level of the morphological paradigm. At each stage of learning, the current grammar is used to find the underlying form for morphemes that yields the maximum-Harmony structural descriptions for paradigms. We provided a miniature example of how this can work in the face of phonological alternation.

Taken as a whole, we have developed and illustrated a proposal for how a learner, provided with the universal elements of any OT UG system, and the overt parts of forms grammatical with respect to some grammar admitted by that UG, could learn the grammar, the structural descriptions, and the lexicon. This proposal decomposes the problem into three subproblems: robust interpretive parsing, lexicon learning, and grammar learning. Currently, we have a set of formal results on the grammar learning subproblem, formal results on the robust interpretive parsing subproblem for interesting classes of OT grammars, and empirical computer experimental results on the simultaneous learning of the grammar and the structural descriptions.

How do these learnability considerations relate to OT work on actual acquisition? We have considered the question of the initial state and reviewed a subset-type argument that uses the OT principle of richness of the base to show that in general Faithfulness constraints must be low ranked in the initial state if unmarked inventories are to be learnable. The concept of robust interpretive parsing developed here makes sense of the proposal that children's inputs are essentially the correct adult forms. This connects a fundamental principle of OT and learnability considerations to two important assumptions of much OT research on phonological acquisition: initial low ranking of Faithfulness and the hypothesis that children's inputs closely approximate the adult forms.

And finally, how does the emerging OT learning theory relate to linguistic explanation? We observed that in OT, constraint interaction is simultaneously the key to both linguistic explanation and learnability: constraint conflict, resolved by language-specific ranking, provides both the explanatory power of OT as a linguistic theory, and the evidence learners need to home in on their target grammar.

How, exactly, does a theory of grammar bear on questions of learnability? This work provides evidence that OT's claims about the structure of UG have manifold implications for learning. The claim that constraints are universal entails that the learner can use a given set of constraints to evaluate structural descriptions. The claim that grammatical structures are optimal, and grammars are total rankings of violable constraints, entails that with every piece of explicit positive evidence comes a mass of implicit negative evidence, and that constraints can be ranked so that those violated by positive data are dominated by those violated by implicit negative data. The claim that grammars are evaluators of structural descriptions provides a uniform basis for the problems of parsing overt forms to determine their hidden structure, parsing inputs to determine their grammatical output, and deducing new inputs for insertion into the lexicon: these are merely three different directions of accessing the evaluative structure that is the grammar. The claim of richness of the base connects the OT basis for adult typologies with fundamental hypotheses underlying acquisition research.

All these implications follow not from a particular OT theory of stress, nor an OT theory of phonology, but from the fundamental structure that OT claims to be inherent in all of grammar. Our learning algorithms derive from this general grammatical structure alone, and so apply to the learning of any OT grammar. At the same time, our algorithms are not generic search procedures, uninformed by a theory of grammar, equally applicable to the problem of learning to classify submarines. The special, characteristically linguistic, structure imposed by OT on UG is sufficiently strong to allow the proof of learnability theorems that state that large spaces of possible grammars can be efficiently navigated to home in on a correct grammar.

7 Correctness and Data Complexity of Constraint Demotion

The formal analysis of Constraint Demotion learning proceeds as follows. A language L is presumed, which is generated by some total ranking. Section 7.1 sets up the basic machinery of stratified constraint hierarchies. Section 7.2 identifies, for any language L, a distinguished stratified hierarchy that generates it, the *target hierarchy* $\mathcal{H}_L$. Section 7.3 defines Constraint Demotion. The case where all constraints are initially top ranked is analyzed first, and CD is shown to converge to the target hierarchy. A distance metric between hierarchies is defined, and it is shown that CD monotonically reduces the distance between the working hypothesis hierarchy and the target, decreasing the distance by at least one unit for each informative example. The maximum number of informative examples needed for learning is thus bounded by the distance between the initial hierarchy and the target. Section 7.4 extends the results to arbitrary initial constraint hierarchies. Section 7.5 demonstrates the adequacy of production-directed parsing for selecting competitors, proving that EDCD will converge to a hierarchy consistent with all positive data presented. Section 7.6 discusses Recursive Constraint Demotion, which is of considerable practical value to the working linguist for automatically ranking constraints, or determining that no ranking exists that is consistent with a body of data.

7.1 Stratified Hierarchies

(7.1) DEFINITION   A stratum is a set of constraints. A stratified hierarchy is a linearly ordered set of strata that partitions the universal constraints. A hierarchy distinguishes one stratum as the top stratum. Each stratum other than the top stratum is immediately dominated by exactly one other stratum. The top stratum immediately dominates the second stratum, which immediately dominates the third stratum, and so forth.

(7.2) DEFINITION   A *total ranking* is a stratified hierarchy where each stratum contains precisely one constraint.

(7.3) DEFINITION   A constraint $\mathbb{C}_1$ is said to dominate constraint $\mathbb{C}_2$, denoted $\mathbb{C}_1 \gg \mathbb{C}_2$, in hierarchy $\mathcal{H}$ if the stratum containing $\mathbb{C}_1$ dominates the stratum containing $\mathbb{C}_2$ in hierarchy $\mathcal{H}$.

(7.4) DEFINITION   The *offset* of a constraint $\mathbb{C}$ in a hierarchy $\mathcal{H}$ is the number of strata that dominate the stratum containing $\mathbb{C}$. $\mathbb{C}$ is *in a lower stratum* in $\mathcal{H}_1$ than in $\mathcal{H}_2$ if the offset of $\mathbb{C}$ in $\mathcal{H}_1$ is greater than in $\mathcal{H}_2$. $\mathbb{C}$ is *in the same stratum* in $\mathcal{H}_1$ and $\mathcal{H}_2$ if it has the same offset in both.

(7.5) DEFINITION   A constraint hierarchy $\mathcal{H}_1$ *h-dominates* $\mathcal{H}_2$ if each constraint $\mathbb{C}$ is in the same or a lower stratum in $\mathcal{H}_2$ than in $\mathcal{H}_1$.

(7.6) DEFINITION   A constraint hierarchy $\mathcal{H}_2$ is called a *refinement* of $\mathcal{H}_1$ if every domination relation $\mathbb{C} \gg \mathbb{C}'$ of $\mathcal{H}_1$ is preserved in $\mathcal{H}_2$.

(7.7) DEFINITION $\mathcal{H}_0$ denotes the stratified hierarchy with all of the constraints in the top stratum.

(7.8) LEMMA $\mathcal{H}_0$ h-dominates all hierarchies.

Proof $\mathcal{H}_0$ h-dominates itself, because h-domination is reflexive (h-domination is satisfied by constraints that are in the same stratum in both hierarchies). Consider some constraint $\mathbb{C}$ in some hierarchy $\mathcal{H}$. $\mathbb{C}$ is either in the top stratum of $\mathcal{H}$, and thus in the same stratum as in $\mathcal{H}_0$, or it is in some lower stratum of $\mathcal{H}$, and thus in a lower stratum than in $\mathcal{H}_0$. Therefore, $\mathcal{H}_0$ h-dominates all hierarchies. ❏

7.2   The Target Stratified Hierarchy

(7.9) DEFINITION   The *h-dominant target stratified hierarchy*, or simply the *target*, for a language L generated by a total ranking, is denoted $\mathcal{H}_L$ and is defined as follows. The top stratum of the target contains precisely those constraints that never assess uncanceled marks to any optimal structural description in L. The second stratum consists of precisely those constraints that assess uncanceled marks only to optimal parses relative to competitors that are assessed at least one uncanceled mark by a constraint in the top stratum. Each stratum consists of precisely those constraints that (a) cannot occur higher in the target, and (b) only assess uncanceled marks to optimal parses relative to competitors assessed an uncanceled mark by at least one constraint ranked higher in the target.

(7.10) LEMMA   For any L generated by a total ranking, $\mathcal{H}_L$ exists and is unique.

Proof   Existence follows from the definition, and the assumption that L is generated by at least one total ranking of the constraints. The top stratum of $\mathcal{H}_L$ is guaranteed to contain at least the constraint ranked highest in the total ranking. Among the constraints not placed in the top stratum of $\mathcal{H}_L$, one dominates all the remaining others in the total ranking, and is thus guaranteed to meet the requirements for placement in the second stratum. The same logic, applied to subsequent strata, shows that all the constraints will be placed in a stratum in $\mathcal{H}_L$.

Uniqueness is guaranteed because a constraint cannot meet the requirements for placement in more than one stratum in the hierarchy, because meeting the requirements for one stratum automatically disqualifies it for any lower strata. ❐

(7.11)   LEMMA   Each constraint $\mathbb{C}$ with offset $n > 0$ in $\mathcal{H}_L$ for a language generated by a total ranking has the following property. There must exist an optimal description *winner* with a competing suboptimal description *loser* such that $\mathbb{C}$ assesses an uncanceled mark to the winner, the loser is assessed an uncanceled mark by a constraint $\mathbb{C}_{n-1}$ with offset precisely $n - 1$, and the loser is not assessed any uncanceled marks by any constraints with offset less than $n - 1$.

Proof   Consider some constraint $\mathbb{C}_n$ with offset $n > 0$ in target $\mathcal{H}_L$. Suppose, to the contrary, that no such loser/winner pair exists for $\mathbb{C}_n$. Recall that if $\mathbb{C}_n$ assesses an uncanceled mark to an optimal description relative to some suboptimal competitor, it must be dominated by some other constraint that assesses an uncanceled mark to the suboptimal competitor, for otherwise the optimal description would not be more harmonic, and the correct language would not be generated.

One possibility is that $\mathbb{C}_n$ never assesses an uncanceled mark to any optimal description. But then it would have offset 0 in $\mathcal{H}_L$, contradicting the assumption that it has offset greater than 0.

The other possibility is that for any winner assessed an uncanceled mark by $\mathbb{C}_n$ relative to some loser, the loser is assessed an uncanceled mark by a constraint with offset smaller than $n - 1$. But then $\mathbb{C}_n$ could be placed one stratum higher in $\mathcal{H}_L$, with resulting offset $n - 1$, and the resulting hierarchy would generate the same language, contradicting the fact that by definition every constraint is ranked as high as possible in $\mathcal{H}_L$.

Hence the supposition must be false, and an appropriate pair must exist. ❐

(7.12)   THEOREM   For any language L generated by a total ranking, $\mathcal{H}_L$ generates L. $\mathcal{H}_L$ also has the property that each constraint is ranked as high as possible; that is, $\mathcal{H}_L$ h-dominates every total ranking $\mathcal{H}'$ that generates L.

Proof Consider some description *winner* in L, and any competitor *loser* with nonidentical marks. If the winner has no uncanceled marks, it is more harmonic than the loser. If the winner has an uncanceled mark, its corresponding constraint must be dominated in $\mathcal{H}_L$ by some constraint assessing an uncanceled mark to *loser*, by the definition of $\mathcal{H}_L$. So $\mathcal{H}_L$ generates L.

For the second part, consider a total ranking $\mathcal{H}'$ that generates L.

Consider a constraint $\mathbb{C}$ with offset 0 in $\mathcal{H}'$. $\mathbb{C}$ must not assess an uncanceled mark to any optimal description in the language; otherwise, $\mathcal{H}'$ would not generate the language. Therefore, $\mathbb{C}$ must have offset 0 in $\mathcal{H}_L$. It follows that $\mathbb{C}$'s offset in $\mathcal{H}_L$ is $\leq$ $\mathbb{C}$'s offset in $\mathcal{H}'$, since both are 0.

Assume that each constraint with offset $\leq n$ in $\mathcal{H}'$ is in the same or higher stratum in $\mathcal{H}_L$. Consider the constraint $\mathbb{C}_{n+1}$ with offset $n+1$ in $\mathcal{H}'$. For any pair of an optimal description *winner* with a suboptimal competitor *loser*, if $\mathbb{C}_{n+1}$ assesses an uncanceled mark to the winner, the loser must be assessed an uncanceled mark by a constraint $\mathbb{C}$ with offset $\leq n$ in $\mathcal{H}'$ (that is, $\mathbb{C} \gg \mathbb{C}_{n+1}$ in $\mathcal{H}'$); otherwise, $\mathcal{H}'$ would not generate the language. By hypothesis, any constraint with offset $\leq n$ in $\mathcal{H}'$ has offset $\leq n$ in $\mathcal{H}_L$. Therefore, $\mathbb{C}_{n+1}$ has offset $\leq n + 1$ in $\mathcal{H}_L$.

By mathematical induction, every constraint in $\mathcal{H}'$ is in the same or higher stratum in $\mathcal{H}_L$. It follows directly that every constraint is in the same or a lower stratum in $\mathcal{H}'$ than in $\mathcal{H}_L$. Therefore, target $\mathcal{H}_L$ h-dominates $\mathcal{H}'$. ❏

(7.13) COROLLARY Every total ranking that is a refinement of $\mathcal{H}_L$ generates L.

Proof By the definition of $\mathcal{H}_L$ (7.9), for every loser/winner pair of L, each uncanceled winner mark is dominated, with respect to $\mathcal{H}_L$, by an uncanceled loser mark. By the definition of refinement (7.6), any refinement of $\mathcal{H}_L$ preserves all such domination relations of $\mathcal{H}_L$. Therefore, any refinement that is a total ranking generates L. ❏

7.3 Constraint Demotion

(7.14) DEFINITION The Mark Cancelation procedure.
Given: Constraint violation marks *marks(loser)* and *marks(winner)*.

Mark_Cancelation(*marks*(*loser*), *marks*(*winner*))
marks′(*loser*) := *marks*(*loser*)
marks′(*winner*) := *marks*(*winner*)
for each occurrence of *$\mathbb{C}$ in both *marks′*(*loser*) and *marks′*(*winner*)
   remove that occurrence of *$\mathbb{C}$ from both lists
end-for
return (*marks′*(*loser*), *marks′*(*winner*))

(7.15)   DEFINITION   The Constraint Demotion procedure.
Given: a mark-data pair (*marks′*(*loser*), *marks′*(*winner*)) after Mark
Cancelation, and a constraint hierarchy $\mathcal{H}$-*start*.
CD((*marks′*(*loser*), *marks′*(*winner*)), $\mathcal{H}$-*start*)
$\mathcal{H}′$:= $\mathcal{H}$-*start*
find the constraint $\mathbb{C}_l$ with a mark in *marks′*(*loser*) ranked highest in
$\mathcal{H}′$
for each $\mathbb{C}_w$ with a mark in *marks′*(*winner*)
   if ($\mathbb{C}_l$ does not dominate $\mathbb{C}_w$ in $\mathcal{H}′$)
      demote $\mathbb{C}_w$ to the stratum immediately below $\mathbb{C}_l$
   end-if
end-for
return($\mathcal{H}′$)

(7.16)   LEMMA   The hierarchy output by CD is h-dominated by the
input hierarchy.

Proof   Because CD only demotes constraints, each constraint is in
either the same or a lower stratum in the output hierarchy than it was
in the input hierarchy. ◻

(7.17)   LEMMA   If the input hierarchy h-dominates $\mathcal{H}_L$, so does the
output hierarchy.

Proof   This holds because CD will never demote a constraint lower than
necessary. Let $\mathbb{C}_w$ be some constraint demoted by CD. Then there is a
mark-data pair (*marks′*(*loser*), *marks′*(*winner*)) requiring that $\mathbb{C}_w$ be
dominated by one of the constraints assessing uncanceled marks to the
loser. Let $\mathbb{C}_l$ be the one with the smallest offset (highest ranked) in
$\mathcal{H}$, the input hierarchy, and let n denote its offset. By assumption, $\mathcal{H}$ h-
dominates $\mathcal{H}_L$, so $\mathbb{C}_l$ in $\mathcal{H}_L$ has offset $\geq n$. Thus, every constraint assessing an uncanceled mark to the loser must have offset $\geq$ n. Therefore, $\mathbb{C}_w$

must have offset at least $n + 1$ in $\mathcal{H}_L$. CD demotes $\mathbb{C}_w$ to the stratum immediately below the one containing $\mathbb{C}_l$, so $\mathbb{C}_w$ has offset $n + 1$ in the resulting hierarchy. Thus, $\mathbb{C}_w$ has offset in the output hierarchy less than or equal to its offset in $\mathcal{H}_L$, guaranteeing that the output hierarchy h-dominates $\mathcal{H}_L$. $\Box$

(7.18) DEFINITION An *informative pair* for a hierarchy $\mathcal{H}'$ is a mark-data pair that, when given as input to CD along with $\mathcal{H}'$, causes at least one demotion to occur. The property of being informative is jointly determined by the mark-data pair and the hierarchy being evaluated.

(7.19) DEFINITION The *h-distance* between a hierarchy $\mathcal{H}_1$ and a hierarchy $\mathcal{H}_2$ h-dominated by $\mathcal{H}_1$ is the sum, over all constraints $\mathbb{C}$, of the difference between the offset of $\mathbb{C}$ in $\mathcal{H}_2$ and in $\mathcal{H}_1$.

(7.20) LEMMA Suppose the input hierarchy h-dominates $\mathcal{H}_L$. The *h-distance* between the output hierarchy and $\mathcal{H}_L$ is decreased by at least one (from the h-distance between the input hierarchy and $\mathcal{H}_L$) for each demotion.

Proof By lemma (7.16), the input hierarchy h-dominates the output hierarchy. Let $\mathbb{C}$ be a constraint that is demoted, with offset n in the input hierarchy, offset m in the output hierarchy, and offset t in $\mathcal{H}_L$. $\mathbb{C}$ is demoted, so $m > n$. By lemma (7.17), the output hierarchy h-dominates $\mathcal{H}_L$, so $t \geq m > n$. Therefore, $(t - m) < (t - n)$, so the contribution of $\mathbb{C}$ to h-distance is smaller for the output hierarchy. Thus, the output hierarchy h-distance is at least one less for each constraint demoted. $\Box$

(7.21) LEMMA Let N be the number of constraints. The h-distance from $\mathcal{H}_0$ to $\mathcal{H}_L$ cannot exceed $\frac{1}{2}(N - 1)N$.

Proof By lemma (7.8), $\mathcal{H}_0$ h-dominates every hierarchy, and therefore must h-dominate $\mathcal{H}_L$. The greatest h-distance will be when $\mathcal{H}_L$ is a totally ranked hierarchy. The furthest constraint from the top stratum will be the one in the bottom stratum, which has offset $(N - 1)$. The next lowest constraint has offset $(N - 2)$, and so forth. Thus, the h-distance will be: $(N - 1) + (N - 2) + \cdots + 1 + 0$, which is precisely $\frac{1}{2}(N - 1)N$. $\Box$

(7.22) THEOREM Starting with $\mathcal{H}_0$ and repeatedly presenting CD with mark-data pairs, the target hierarchy $\mathcal{H}_L$ is converged on after at most $\frac{1}{2}(N - 1)N$ informative pairs.

Proof By lemma (7.20), each informative pair reduces the h-distance by at least one. Therefore the target hierarchy is converged on after a number of informative pairs that is at most the h-distance between $\mathcal{H}_0$ and the target. Lemma (7.21) guarantees that this distance is at most $\frac{1}{2}(N-1)N$. □

7.4 Extension to Arbitrary Initial Hierarchies

We now consider CD starting from some arbitrary initial hierarchy, denoted $\mathcal{H}_0$. K denotes the maximal offset in $\mathcal{H}_0$ (one less than the number of strata, since the offset of the top stratum is zero). A slight elaboration of CD is made: If the last constraint in a stratum gets demoted, for bookkeeping purposes the empty stratum is retained in the hierarchy. That way, the offset (stratum number) of all the constraints that are not demoted will be unaffected (empty strata can occur when starting with an arbitrary initial hierarchy, but not when starting with all constraints top ranked).

With an arbitrary initial hierarchy, the target hierarchy $\mathcal{H}_L$ is not the exact goal of learning. Instead, it is used to define a new hierarchy $\mathcal{H}^\#$ that CD approaches and can never go beyond. As before, this bound on demotion makes it possible to compute a limit to the number of demotions possible before a correct solution is reached.

(7.23) DEFINITION The offset of constraint $\mathbb{C}$ in hierarchy $\mathcal{H}$ is denoted $v(\mathbb{C},\mathcal{H})$.

(7.24) DEFINITION The *lower bounding hierarchy* for L, $\mathcal{H}^\#$, is the stratified hierarchy in which the first K strata are empty, and then a copy of $\mathcal{H}_L$ runs from the stratum with offset K down. That is, the offset of any constraint $\mathbb{C}$ in $\mathcal{H}^\#$ is K more than its offset in $\mathcal{H}_L$: $v(\mathbb{C},\mathcal{H}^\#) = K + v(\mathbb{C},\mathcal{H}_L)$.

(7.25) DEFINITION During the operation of the CD algorithm, let D denote the h-distance (7.19) between the algorithm's current stratified hierarchy $\mathcal{H}$ and the lower bounding hierarchy $\mathcal{H}^\#$: $D \equiv \Sigma_\mathbb{C} \, [v(\mathbb{C},\mathcal{H}^\#) - v(\mathbb{C},\mathcal{H})]$

(7.26) LEMMA For each loser/winner pair of L in which $*\mathbb{C}$ is an uncanceled winner mark, $\mathbb{C}$ is dominated in $\mathcal{H}_L$ by some $\mathbb{C}'$ such that $*\mathbb{C}'$ is an uncanceled loser mark.

Proof $\mathcal{H}_L$ correctly accounts for all the data in L (7.12) so in any loser/winner pair each uncanceled winner mark must be dominated by an uncanceled loser mark. ❐

(7.27) LEMMA   The CD algorithm never demotes $\mathbb{C}$ below the stratum with offset $v(\mathbb{C},\mathcal{H}^{\#})$.

Proof By induction on $v(\mathbb{C},\mathcal{H}_L)$, the offset of $\mathbb{C}$ in $\mathcal{H}_L$.
Let $\mathbb{C}$ be a constraint in the top stratum of $\mathcal{H}_L$, with $v(\mathbb{C},\mathcal{H}_L) = 0$. Then $\mathbb{C}$ will never be demoted by CD. This is so because, by the definition of CD, such demotion would require that $*\mathbb{C}$ be an uncanceled mark of a winner, which is impossible for a constraint in the top stratum of $\mathcal{H}_L$. Thus for each constraint $\mathbb{C}$ with $v(\mathbb{C},\mathcal{H}_L) = 0$, $\mathbb{C}$ is never demoted by CD, and remains in whatever stratum it happens to occupy in $\mathcal{H}_0$. The lowest stratum in $\mathcal{H}_0$ has offset K, so a constraint $\mathbb{C}$ with $v(\mathbb{C},\mathcal{H}_L) = 0$ ends up where it starts, in a stratum with offset at most $K + 0 = K + v(\mathbb{C},\mathcal{H}_L) \equiv v(\mathbb{C},\mathcal{H}^{\#})$. This establishes the base case for the induction.
   Now for the inductive step we assume that for all constraints $\mathbb{C}$ with $v(\mathbb{C},\mathcal{H}_L) < k$, the CD algorithm never demotes $\mathbb{C}$ below offset $v(\mathbb{C},\mathcal{H}^{\#})$. Let $\mathbb{C}$ be a constraint with $v(\mathbb{C},\mathcal{H}_L) = k$. By lemma (7.26), for each loser/winner pair in which $*\mathbb{C}$ is an uncanceled winner mark, $\mathbb{C}$ is dominated in $\mathcal{H}_L$ by some $\mathbb{C}'$ such that $\mathbb{C}'$ is an uncanceled loser mark. This implies that $\mathbb{C}'$ has a lower offset than $\mathbb{C}$ in $\mathcal{H}_L$, and it follows that $v(\mathbb{C}',\mathcal{H}_L) < k$. Thus, by the inductive hypothesis, $\mathbb{C}'$ is demoted to a stratum no lower than $v(\mathbb{C}',\mathcal{H}^{\#}) \equiv K + v(\mathbb{C}',\mathcal{H}_L) \leq K + k - 1 = v(\mathbb{C},\mathcal{H}^{\#}) - 1$. Each time $\mathbb{C}$ is demoted (due to an error on a loser/winner pair in which $*\mathbb{C}$ is an uncanceled winner mark), it is demoted to just below the highest stratum containing a $\mathbb{C}'$ such that $*\mathbb{C}'$ is an uncanceled loser mark. We are guaranteed by induction that such a $\mathbb{C}'$ is to be found among the top $v(\mathbb{C},\mathcal{H}^{\#}) - 1$ strata, so $\mathbb{C}$ cannot be demoted below stratum $v(\mathbb{C},\mathcal{H}^{\#})$. And $\mathbb{C}$ cannot *start* below this stratum either, since $v(\mathbb{C},\mathcal{H}^{\#}) \geq K$, and no constraint starts lower than K. This completes the inductive step. ❐

(7.28) LEMMA D can never go negative. D monotonically decreases during the execution of CD.

Proof That D is never negative now follows immediately since all the terms in the sum defining it are nonnegative, by lemma (7.27). That D

monotonically decreases during the execution of CD is obvious, since CD only demotes constraints, which can only decrease D. ❐

(7.29) THEOREM   CD converges to a hierarchy generating L after no more than $N(N-1)$ informative examples.

Proof By lemma (7.28), the number of demotions cannot exceed the initial value of D: each demotion decreases D by at least 1, and D can never go negative. How large can the initial value of D be? In the worst case, the final hierarchy is totally ranked and the initial hierarchy is the exact inverse of the final hierarchy. In this case, $K = N - 1$, and the initially top-ranked constraint must be demoted $2K$ strata, the constraint below it must be demoted $2(K - 1)$ strata, and so on, with the initially lowest-ranked constraint not being demoted at all, and ending up top ranked. The total number of strata passed through, D, in this worst case is thus twice the corresponding sum in the case where all constraints are initially top ranked (7.21):

$$
\begin{aligned}
2K + 2(K-1) + \cdots + 0 &= 2(N-1) + 2(N-2) + \cdots + 0 \\
&= 2[(N-1) + (N-2) + \cdots + 0] \\
&= 2\left[\frac{1}{2}N(N-1)\right] \\
&= N(N-1)
\end{aligned}
$$

After the last demotion, at latest after $N(N-1)$ informative examples, the fact that there are no more demotions means that there are no more remaining informative examples. If the hierarchy did not generate L, there would exist further informative examples, and by assumption the learner would receive them and make further demotions. ❐

7.5   Error-Driven Constraint Demotion

(7.30) DEFINITION   The Error-Driven Constraint Demotion algorithm. Given: A set *positive-data* of grammatical structural descriptions, and a constraint hierarchy ℋ-*start*.
EDCD(*positive-data*, ℋ-*start*)
ℋ := ℋ-*start*
for each description *winner* in *positive-data*

```
repeat
    input := the underlying form of winner
    loser := the optimal description of input, using ℋ
    if (loser is not identical to winner)
        md := (marks(loser), marks(winner))
        md-canceled := Mark_Cancelation(md)
        ℋ-new := CD(md-canceled, ℋ)
        ℋ := ℋ-new
    end-if
    until (loser is identical to winner)
end-for
return (ℋ)
```

(7.31) THEOREM   EDCD converges to a hierarchy consistent with all positive evidence from L, and converges after at most $N(N-1)$ informative examples.

Proof   The theorem follows directly from theorem (7.29), and the fact that, for any observed winner, if the learner's hypothesized hierarchy does not find the winner optimal, production-directed parsing will produce a competitor guaranteed to result in at least one demotion when CD is applied. ❐

Theorem (7.31) states that EDCD converges to a hierarchy consistent with all positive evidence from L, rather than a hierarchy generating L, for the following reason: If different grammars have subset relations, where the language generated by one grammar is a strict subset of the language generated by another, then EDCD, when given positive evidence from a subset language, may converge on a superset language, consistent with all the positive evidence but not generating the same language. The outcome may depend on the starting hierarchy, among other factors; see section 5.1. This subset sensitivity is a consequence of the error-driven nature of EDCD combined with only positive evidence; if the appropriate loser/winner pairs were obtained, the CD principle itself, properly applied, would guarantee convergence to the (correct) subset language.

7.6   Recursive Constraint Demotion

The Recursive Constraint Demotion algorithm is first exemplified using CVT. A general definition and analysis of the algorithm is then provided.

7.6.1   The Recursive Constraint Demotion (RCD) Algorithm: An Example

The starting point is the initial data, a set of loser/winner mark-data pairs, with common marks canceled. For our CV language L_1, these data are given in table 3.3, and in tableau form in table 3.2; they are repeated here as tables 7.1 and 7.2.

After Mark Cancelation, the remainder of the algorithm proceeds recursively, finding first the constraints that may be ranked highest while being consistent with the mark-data pairs, then eliminating those constraints from the problem and starting over again to rank the remaining, lower, constraints. Conceived as a sequence of passes, the first pass through the data determines the highest-ranking constraints, the next

Table 7.1

Mark-data pairs after cancelation (L_1)

	loser/winner pairs			*marks'(loser)*	*marks'(winner)*
(a) ≺ (d)	.V.CVC.	≺	□V.CV.⟨C⟩	*ONSET *NOCODA	*PARSE *FILL^{Ons}
(b) ≺ (d)	⟨V⟩.CV.⟨C⟩	≺	.□V.CV.⟨C⟩	~~*PARSE~~ *PARSE	~~*PARSE~~ *FILL^{Ons}
(c) ≺ (d)	⟨V⟩.CV.C□.	≺	.□V.CV.⟨C⟩	~~*PARSE~~ *FILL^{Nuc}	~~*PARSE~~ *FILL^{Ons}

Table 7.2
Initial data in tableau form (L_1)

loser/winner pairs		*not-yet-ranked*				
		FILL^{Nuc}	FILL^{Ons}	PARSE	ONSET	NOCODA
(d) ✓	.□V.CV.⟨C⟩		⊛	⊛		
(a)	.V.CVC.				*	*
(d) ✓	.□V.CV.⟨C⟩		⊛	⊠		
(b)	⟨V⟩.CV.⟨C⟩			⊠ *		
(d) ✓	.□V.CV.⟨C⟩		⊛	⊠		
(c)	⟨V⟩.CV.C□.	*		⊠		

pass the next-highest-ranking constraints, and so forth down the hierarchy. If the data provide enough information to completely determine
the total ranking, only one constraint will be returned by each pass.
In general, however, the result of the algorithm will be a stratified
hierarchy.

When the algorithm begins, the not-yet-ranked constraints comprise
the entire universal set (2.6):

not-yet-ranked-constraints
    $= \{$ONSET, NoCODA, PARSE, FILL^{Nuc}, FILL$^{\text{Ons}}\}$

Examining the rightmost column of the mark-data table, table 7.1, we
see that two marks, *PARSE and *FILL^{Ons}, appear in the list of uncanceled
winner marks: these are the constraints whose columns in table 7.2
contain uncanceled ⊛ marks. So the two constraints PARSE and FILL^{Ons}
must be dominated by other constraints (those violated by the corresponding losers); they cannot be the highest ranked of the *not-yet-
ranked-constraints*. The remaining constraints, on the other hand, *can* be
top ranked, because they assess no uncanceled marks to any winners.
Thus:

(7.32)   *highest-ranked-constraints* = {ONSET, NoCODA, FILL^{Nuc}}

This constitutes the output of the first pass: these three constraints
form the highest stratum in the hierarchy. The data do not support any
distinctions in ranking among the three, so none are made. Now,

(7.33)   *not-yet-ranked-constraints* = {PARSE, FILL^{Ons}}

The result of the first pass is shown in tableau form in table 7.3. The
columns with uncanceled winner marks ⊛ have been demoted below
those without; this is all there is to it.

Now that the highest-ranked constraints have been determined, the
list of mark-data pairs can be trimmed down by removing any mark-data
pairs that are completely accounted for by the constraints selected as
highest. This is the case if at least one of the marks incurred by the loser
of a pair is among the highest-ranked constraints. Such a mark is guaranteed to dominate all the corresponding winner's marks, because all of
the winner's marks were disqualified from being ranked highest. In the
tableau of table 7.3, we see that (d) is now more harmonic than (a), which

Table 7.3
Hierarchy after pass one

winner/loser pairs			already-ranked			not-yet-ranked	
			FILL^{Nuc}	ONSET	NOCODA	FILL^{Ons}	PARSE
(d)	☞ ✓	.□V.CV.⟨C⟩				⊛	⊛
(a)		.V.CVC.		*!	*!		
(d)	✓	.□V.CV.⟨C⟩				⊛	⊠
(b)		⟨V⟩.CV.⟨C⟩					⊠ *
(d)	☞✓	.□V.CV.⟨C⟩				⊛	⊠
(c)		⟨V⟩.CV.C⌷.	*!				⊠

earns two fatal uncanceled marks in the top stratum; these marks render irrelevant the winner marks in the lower stratum, as shown by the gray shading. Similarly, (d) is more harmonic than (c). But the hierarchy at this point does not yet make (d) more harmonic than (b): their two PARSE marks cancel, and the second PARSE mark of (b) equals the FILL^{Ons} mark of (d), since these two constraints are currently equally ranked.

So to proceed to further ranking, we eliminate from the mark-data table those winner/loser pairs that are now accounted for; this amounts to eliminating every row in which any of the highest-ranked constraints appear. So we eliminate the pair (a) < (d) because *ONSET appears (or, alternatively, because *NOCODA appears), and also the pair (c) < (d), because *FILL^{Nuc} appears. The new mark-data table is represented as table 7.4.

In tableau form, the remaining data pair is shown in table 7.5.

At the end of the first pass, we now have the first (highest) stratum (7.32), and a reduced list of not-yet-ranked constraints (7.33), and a reduced mark-data table, table 7.5. Crucially, the reduced mark-data table involves only the *not-yet-ranked-constraints*, so we can now recursively invoke the same algorithm, using the remaining data to rank the remaining constraints. This initiates the next pass.

Repeating this process with the reduced mark-data table—table 7.5— we examine the rightmost column of the table, and observe that of the two *not-yet-ranked-constraints* (7.33), only one, FILL^{Ons}, appears. The remaining constraint, then, is output as the next stratum of highest-ranked constraints:

Table 7.4
Mark-data pairs (L_1, after first pass)

subopt ≺ opt		loser-marks	winner-marks
(b) ≺ (d)	$\langle V \rangle$.CV.$\langle C \rangle$ ≺ □V.CV.$\langle C \rangle$	*~~Parse~~ *Parse	*~~Parse~~ Fill^{Ons}

Table 7.5
Data after first pass

		already-ranked			not-yet-ranked	
winner/loser pairs		Fill^{Nuc}	Onset	NoCoda	Fill^{Ons}	Parse
(d) ✓	□V.CV.$\langle C \rangle$				⊛	⊠
(b)	$\langle V \rangle$.CV.$\langle C \rangle$					⊠ *

Table 7.6
After second pass

		already-ranked				not-yet-ranked
winner/loser pairs		Fill^{Nuc}	Onset	NoCoda	Parse	Fill^{Ons}
(d) ☞✓	□V.CV.$\langle C \rangle$				⊠	⊛
(b)	$\langle V \rangle$.CV.$\langle C \rangle$				⊠ *!	

(7.34)   *highest-ranked-constraints* = {Parse}

This leaves

(7.35)   *not-yet-ranked-constraints* = {Fill^{Ons}}

In tableau form, the column with the winner mark ⊛ is demoted, ensuring that (d) is more harmonic than (b) (see table 7.6).

The final step of the second pass is to trim the mark-data table, eliminating rows in which the *highest-ranked-constraints* appear. This eliminates the only row in the table, so that the new mark-data table is empty.

(7.36)   Mark-data pairs (L_1, after second pass): none

The result of the first two passes is the highest segment of the stratified hierarchy:

$\{\text{ONSET}, \text{NOCODA}, \text{FILL}^{\text{Nuc}}\} \gg \{\text{PARSE}\}$

The third pass operates on an empty mark-data table. Since there are no marks in the rightmost column of such a table, no remaining constraints must be dominated: all the not-yet-ranked constraints are output as the highest ranked. In this case, that is the one remaining constraint FILL^{Ons}.

(7.37)   *highest-ranked-constraints* = $\{\text{FILL}^{\text{Ons}}\}$

This leaves

(7.38)   *not-yet-ranked-constraints* = $\{\}$

so the algorithm terminates, with the final result:

(7.39)   Learned Stratified Hierarchy for L_1:
$\{\text{ONSET}, \text{NOCODA}, \text{FILL}^{\text{Nuc}}\} \gg \{\text{PARSE}\} \gg \{\text{FILL}^{\text{Ons}}\}$

This result represents a class of totally ranked constraint hierarchies all of which give rise to the target language L_1: the same optimal outputs arise regardless of the ranking of the three highest constraints. One of these refinements of the learned stratified hierarchy (7.39) is the particular total ranking given in (2.11): this is but one of the correct hierarchies for the target language.

The final result is shown in tableau form in table 7.7, where it may be verified that every winner/loser pair is now correctly accounted for by the hierarchy.

Table 7.7
Learned hierarchy for L_1 and learning data

	winner/loser pairs	FILL^{Nuc}	ONSET	NOCODA	PARSE	FILL^{Ons}
			already-ranked			
(d) ☞ ✓	.□V.CV.⟨C⟩				⊛	⊛
(a)	.V.CVC.		*!	*!		
(d) ☞ ✓	.□V.CV.⟨C⟩				⊠	⊛
(b)	⟨V⟩.CV.⟨C⟩				⊠	*!
(d) ☞ ✓	.□V.CV.⟨C⟩				⊠	⊛
(c)	⟨V⟩.CV.C□.	*!			⊠	

Table 7.8
Mark-data pairs after cancelation (L_2)

	subopt	≺	opt	loser-marks	winner-marks
(a) ≺ (c)	.V.CVC	≺	⟨V⟩.CV.C◻.	*ONSET *NOCODA	*PARSE *FILL^{Nuc}
(b) ≺ (c)	⟨V⟩.CV.⟨C⟩	≺	⟨V⟩.CV.C◻.	~~*PARSE~~ *PARSE	~~*PARSE~~ *FILL^{Nuc}
(d) ≺ (c)	.◻V.CV.⟨C⟩	≺	⟨V⟩.CV.C◻.	~~*PARSE~~ *FILL^{Ons}	~~*PARSE~~ *FILL^{Nuc}

It is easy to see how the course of learning L_2 differs from that of L_1, assuming the learner's initial datum is the parse of the same input, /VCVC/, which is now ⟨V⟩.CV.C◻. (candidate (c) in (7.2); see the tableau in table 2.4). The mark-data table used by the algorithm, containing the marks of *subopt* ≺ *opt* pairs after cancelation, is shown as table 7.8.

This table is identical to its L_1 counterpart table 7.1 except that the marks *FILL^{Nuc} and *FILL^{Ons} are interchanged. The result of the algorithm is therefore the same as before, (7.39), with this exchange made.

(7.40)   Learned stratified hierarchy for L_2:
{ONSET, NOCODA, FILL^{Ons}} ≫ {PARSE} ≫ {FILL^{Nuc}}

Again, this stratified hierarchy is correct: its further refinements into totally ranked hierarchies, including the one we singled out in (2.12), all give rise to L_2.

That these CV languages can each be learned completely from a single positive example attests to the power of the implicit negative data that comes with each positive example in OT.

7.6.2   General Statement of the RCD Algorithm

Having illustrated the Recursive Constraint Demotion algorithm in the context of CVT, we now formulate the algorithm in full generality.

(7.41)   The grammar learning problem
Given: A set *universal-constraints* of universal constraints, and a set *initial-data* of outputs of the target language L, where L arises from some (not necessarily unique) total ranking of the universal constraints.
To Find: A stratified hierarchy in which each output of *initial-data* is the optimal parse of its corresponding input.

(7.42)   Data Preparation
Given: a set *inital-data* of well-formed outputs of the target language
L, and a set *constraints* of universal constraints.
Data_Preparation (*initial-data*, *constraints*)
create a table *mark-data*, with columns for *loser-marks* and *winner-marks*
for each output *opt* in *initial-data*
  choose a set *competitors* of suboptimal competitors
  for each competitor *subopt* in *competitors*
    create a pair (*marks(subopt)*, *marks(opt)*)
    apply mark cancelation to (*marks(subopt)*, *marks(opt)*)
    add (*marks(subopt)*, *marks(opt)*) to *mark-data*
      put *marks(subopt)* in column *loser-marks*
      put *marks(opt)* in column *winner-marks*
    end-add
  end-for
end-for
return(*mark-data*)

Once prepared, the data are organized in a form illustrated by
table 7.9.

(7.43)   Recursive Constraint Demotion (RCD)
Given: a set *constraints* of universal constraints, and a prepared table
mark-data of mark-data pairs (*loser-marks*, *winner-marks*).
RCD(*constraints*, *mark-data*)
set ℋ-*new* to be an empty hierarchy
not-yet-ranked-constraints := constraints
repeat
  /* Step (a) */

Table 7.9
Learning data take this form

subopt ≺ opt	loser-marks = marks(sub-opt)	winner-marks = marks(opt)
...	...	...

    set *highest-ranked-constraints* to be empty
for each constraint $\mathbb{C}$ in *not-yet-ranked-constraints*
    if (*$\mathbb{C}$ does not appear in *winner-marks*)
        remove $\mathbb{C}$ from *not-yet-ranked-constraints*
        add $\mathbb{C}$ to *highest-ranked-constraints*
    end-if
    end-for
    /* Step (b) */
    for each constraint $\mathbb{C}$ in *highest-ranked-constraints*
    if (*$\mathbb{C}$ appears in a mark-data pair of *mark-data*)
        remove that pair from *mark-data*
    end-if
    end-for
    put *highest-ranked-constraints* as the next stratum in $\mathcal{H}$-*new*
until (*not-yet-ranked-constraints* is empty)
return($\mathcal{H}$-*new*)

Note that in step (b), the relevant marks (those assessed by the *highest-ranked-constraints*) can only appear in the column *loser-marks*; for any constraint contributing a mark to the column *winner-marks* is not, by step (a), among the relevant constraints (those in *highest-ranked-constraints*).

7.6.3 Analysis of the RCD Algorithm

Observe first that multiple uncanceled tokens of the same type of mark in the *mark-data* table, either for winner or loser, have the same effect as a single token. For in step (a), we simply determine which constraints assess no marks at all in the *winner-marks* column: whether a single or multiple tokens of a mark appear makes no difference. Then in step (b), a row is removed from *mark-data* if it contains any marks at all assessed by the *highest-ranked-constraints*; multiple tokens of a mark type have the same effect as a single token. Thus, for efficiency considerations below, we can assume that in Mark Cancelation, if a row of the *mark-data* table contains multiple tokens of the same type of mark after cancelation, duplicates are eliminated, leaving at most one token of each type. In other words, in the initial mark-data table prior to cancelation, what really matters is, for each constraint, which of *subopt* or *opt* incurs more violations of the constraint $\mathbb{C}$; if it is *subopt*, a token of the mark

$*\mathbb{C}$ appears in the column *loser-marks*; if it is *opt*, the token of $*\mathbb{C}$ appears instead in the column *winner-marks*. What matters in the assessment of optimality is only which of two candidates more seriously violates each constraint, not any absolute magnitude of violation (see discussion following (2.9)).

The correctness of the algorithm should be clear. The *highest-ranked-constraints* output at each pass of the algorithm are exactly the constraints that need not be dominated in order to explain the available *data*; the remaining *not-yet-ranked-constraints*, by contrast, must be dominated and so cannot be highest ranked. We now show that the algorithm must terminate.

On each pass of the algorithm, at least one constraint must be output. For suppose not. That would mean that every one of the *not-yet-ranked-constraints* appears in the column *winner-marks*—that is, as an uncanceled mark of an optimal form. But that would mean that every one of the *not-yet-ranked-constraints* must be dominated by one of the other *not-yet-ranked-constraints*, which means there is no ranking of these constraints consistent with the *mark-data*, in contradiction to the basic assumption that the *mark-data* derive from some ranking of the given constraints.

It is worth noting at this point that if the initial data presented to the RCD algorithm are not consistent with any total ranking of the given constraints, the algorithm discovers this fact: at some stage of its execution, it fails at step (a) to find a constraint that does not appear among the *winner-marks*.

So, under the assumption that the data are consistent with some total ranking of the given constraints, on each pass, at least one constraint is eliminated from the *not-yet-ranked-constraints*. Thus the number of passes required cannot be more than the number of universal constraints: call this N_c. The number of steps required for each pass cannot exceed the number of uncanceled marks in the *mark-data* table: each mark in the column *winner-marks* is examined in step (a) to ensure that its corresponding constraint will not be output as a *highest-ranked-constraint*, and, in the worst case, each mark in the column *loser-marks* must be examined in step (c) to determine which rows must be eliminated from *mark-data*. The number of uncanceled marks per row of the table cannot exceed the number of constraints N_c, so the total number of steps per pass cannot exceed $N_c N_p$, where N_p is the number of rows in the initial *mark-data* table—that is, the number of pairs *subopt* < *opt* used.

The number of steps required for all the passes cannot exceed $N_p(N_c)^2$.

Thus the algorithm is quite efficient: in the worst case, the RCD algorithm is quadratic in the number of constraints, and linear in the number of mark-data pairs.

In summary, then, we have established the following result.

(7.44) THEOREM   Correctness and data complexity of Recursive Constraint Demotion

Suppose given a total ranking of N_c constraints in a set *Con*, and N_p data pairs from this ranking, each an optimal structural description of some input paired with a competing parse of the same input. Given this data, the Recursive Constraint Demotion algorithm converges to a stratified constraint hierarchy consistent with the data, the number of operations required being at most $N_p(N_c)^2$.

7.6.4   The Relation of RCD to EDCD

RCD works with a complete list of mark-data pairs all at once. It derives the ranking entirely from that list of mark-data pairs; there is no role to be played by an initial hierarchy of any sort. Of the possible stratified constraint hierarchies consistent with a given set of mark-data pairs, RCD always derives a specific hierarchy, the one in which each constraint is ranked as high as possible. If a given set of mark-data pairs is collectively inconsistent, RCD will conclusively determine that fact.

EDCD works with one mark-data pair at a time. It assumes the existence of a hypothesized working constraint hierarchy at any given time, and modifies it in accordance with whatever mark-data pair it is currently working with. When EDCD proceeds to the next datum, it is using the constraint hierarchy to carry along (indirectly) the information gained from the previous data. Because EDCD maintains a working constraint hierarchy at all times, it is able to use that hierarchy to test new data for mismatches (the error-driven learning), and to automatically generate informative losers (the indirect negative evidence).

To use RCD in an error-driven fashion, the learner would have to maintain a list of all the generated mark-data pairs, and apply RCD to the entire list each time new information is added. In exchange, RCD will detect inconsistency in the data, while EDCD will continuously demote constraints in response to inconsistent data.

8 Production-Directed Parsing

8.1 The Parsing Problem in Optimality Theory

A grammar specifies a function: the grammar itself does not specify an algorithm, it simply assigns a grammatical structural description to each input. However, one can ask the computational question of whether efficient algorithms exist to compute the description assigned to a linguistic input. This is the parsing problem considered here. Although the term *parsing* is more commonly associated with models of language comprehension, we are treating it as the more general issue of assigning structure to input, an issue relevant to both comprehension and production. In fact, the canonical function defined by an OT grammar is more easily thought of as relating to production: the input is an underlying form, and the structural description includes the surface form. Parsing in OT is easily understood as an optimization problem: search the space of candidate structural descriptions for the one that optimally satisfies the ranked constraints.

The general spirit of OT is to generate a large and general space of candidate structural descriptions for an input, leaving much of the work to the constraints to determine grammaticality. This makes the parsing problem nontrivial; *GEN* is often envisioned as generating an infinite number of candidate structural descriptions for an input, in which case simple exhaustive search is not even tenable. Even if *GEN* were finite, the number of candidates would still grow exponentially in the length of the input.

Although OT is easily understood mathematically in terms of the generation and evaluation of all candidates in parallel, it is unnecessary, and in fact counterproductive, to consider the computation of optimal descriptions in those terms. The algorithm presented here uses a technique known as *dynamic programming*. Intuitively, the algorithm operates by gradually constructing a few candidate parses as it works through the input. When the end of the input is reached, only a few complete parses have been constructed, one of which is guaranteed to be optimal. As an illustration, a complete parser is described for CVT (see chapter 2 for a definition of CVT).

8.1.1 An Intuitive Illustration of Dynamic Programming

The fundamental idea underlying dynamic programming is here introduced via an intuitive analogy. Suppose that there are two towns, X and

Y. In between these towns is a river, which must be crossed in order to travel from X to Y. There are three bridges across the river: A, B, and C. Suppose that we wish to find the shortest—the optimal—route from X to Y.

We know that any path between X and Y must cross one of the three bridges. There are several different ways to get from town X to each of the three bridges, and several different ways to get from each of the bridges to town Y. However, we can simplify our problem by first only considering the best way to get from X to A, the best way from X to B, and the best way from X to C. Having found each of these "subroutes," we could make a small table for future reference: it would have three entries, each giving the shortest route (and its distance) to one of the bridges. Next, we could consider the best way to get to Y from each of the three bridges. Once we determine the shortest route from bridge A to town Y, we can easily calculate the shortest route from X to Y that crosses bridge A, by adding the distance of the shortest route from A to Y with the table entry giving the distance from X to A. In the same fashion, we can calculate the shortest route from X to Y crossing B, by combining the shortest route from B to Y and using the already-calculated shortest route from X to B. The same can be done for bridge C. At this point, we need only choose the shortest of three routes: the shortest route of those for each of the three bridges.

Notice that there are many possible routes between X and Y; just considering bridge A, every possible route from X to A may be combined with every possible route from A to Y. In fact, the problem is most appropriately described in that fashion, as the problem of searching the space of all possible routes between X and Y to find the shortest one. But while the problem is most easily stated and understood in those terms, it is not most easily solved in those terms. The above illustration gives the essence of dynamic programming: break a large problem, like traveling from X to Y, into smaller subproblems, like traveling from X to A, and traveling from A to Y.

The value of this way of thinking is perhaps even more apparent if we change the problem so that there are two rivers between X and Y: the second river having three bridges, D, E, and F. In this case, we would first put into our table the shortest route from X to the bridges A, B, and C. Next, for bridge D, we would consider the shortest route from each of the bridges A, B, and C. We would then make another table entry giving the shortest route from town X to bridge D: this will be the shortest of three routes, the shortest route from X to D via bridge A, via bridge B, and via bridge C. Next, similar table entries would be written down for bridges E and F. Finally, we could calculate the shortest route from town X to town Y by considering the shortest route via bridge D, via E, and via F. Again, at the end, we need only compare three complete routes between X and Y.

The algorithm presented here will use dynamic programming to compute optimal descriptions. Each segment of the input is something like a river in the above illustration. There are a limited number of ways to deal with an input segment, and the best way to do each can be recorded in a table. Once all the input segments have been considered in order, only a very few entire parses of the input need be compared to determine the optimal one.

8.2   Formalizing CVT

An input to the grammar is a string of segments categorized as consonants and vowels—that is, a member of $\{C,V\}^+$. The structural descriptions generated by *GEN* are sequences of syllables with the following restrictions: nuclei are mandatory, onsets and codas are optional, and positions are assumed to contain at most one input segment. The order of the input segments must be preserved, and each input segment must either be placed in a single syllabic position or marked as unparsed in the structure. Further, a C may only be parsed as an onset or a coda, while V may only be parsed as a nucleus. Notice that this is a statement of the universal set of structural descriptions to be considered, not the inventory for any particular language. For a given input, *GEN* generates all possible syllable structures that contain the input, and meet the restrictions just given.

The problem of computing the optimal structural description is nontrivial because *GEN* is allowed to underparse and overparse. Because overparsing may in principle occur an unbounded number of times, the space of candidate structural descriptions for any given input is infinite.

For computational purposes, we will regard a structural description of an input as a string of *syllabic positions*, referred to as a *position structure*. The positions are matched with the input segments. The positions are represented by the symbols {*o,n,d*}, for onset, nucleus, and coda, respectively (C is reserved for consonant). In a given structural description, each position may be filled with at most one input segment, and each input segment may be parsed into at most one position. Any input segment not parsed into a syllabic position is so marked in the structural description. For a given position structure, each allowable way of matching the input with the structure counts as a candidate structural description. An allowable matching is one in which the order of the input segments is preserved, and in which V segments are only parsed into *n* positions, while C segments are only parsed into *o* and *d* positions.

I will use the following *position grammar* to describe the set of allowable position structures:

(8.1)   The position grammar
a. S $\Rightarrow$ *e* | *o*O | *n*N
b. O $\Rightarrow$ *n*N
c. N $\Rightarrow$ *e* | *d*D | *o*O | *n*N
d. D $\Rightarrow$ *e* | *o*O | *n*N

The terminals in the position grammar are the syllabic positions and the empty string (*e*). The nonterminals {S, O, N, D} may be thought of as corresponding to states in the derivation of a position structure. S is the starting state. O signifies that the last position generated was an onset (*o*), N that a nucleus (*n*) was just generated, and D a coda (*d*).

(8.2)   S $\Rightarrow$ *n*N $\Rightarrow$ *nd*D $\Rightarrow$ *ndo*O $\Rightarrow$ *ndon*N $\Rightarrow$ *ndon*

Nonterminals that may evaluate to *e* correspond to possible finishing states. O is not a finishing state, because a syllable with an onset must also have a nucleus. This position grammar guarantees that each syllable has a nucleus, that onsets precede nuclei, that codas follow nuclei, and that there is at most one of each type of position per syllable.

It should here be emphasized that the position grammar just discussed is a descriptive formalism useful in understanding *GEN*; it is *not* a computational mechanism. The actual computational mechanism understandable in terms of the position grammar is the set of operations contained in the Operations Set, described below.

8.3   Parsing with CVT

The challenge is to efficiently choose the optimal structural description from an infinite set of candidates. The solution is to avoid dealing with whole structural descriptions, and instead build up the optimal description piece by piece. The basic technique used to do this is dynamic programming (see, e.g., Corman, Leiserson, and Rivest 1990). The algorithm presented here is related to chart parsing (see, e.g., Kay 1980), an algorithm used in natural language parsing that employs dynamic programming in a nonoptimization form. Dynamic programming has also been used for optimization in sequence comparison (see, e.g., Sankoff and Kruskal 1983), Hidden Markov models (for an overview, see Rabiner 1989), and statistical language modeling (for an overview, see Charniak 1993). The approach presented here is similar to the use of dynamic programming in statistical language processing, but with nonprobabilistic optimization.

The algorithm proceeds by creating a table, called the *Dynamic Programming Table*, and filling in the cells of the table. Once all of the cells have been filled, the optimal description is quite easily determined. Section 8.3.1 describes the table and explains how it contributes to computing the optimal description. Section 8.3.2 describes the operations used to fill the cells of the table, both how they relate to the table and how they relate to CVT.

8.3.1   The Dynamic Programming Table

The illustration in this section assumes the constraint ranking shown in (8.3).

(8.3)   ONS $\gg$ NOCODA $\gg$ FILL^{Nuc} $\gg$ PARSE $\gg$ FILL^{Ons}.

Table 8.1 shows the Dynamic Programming (DP) Table for the input /VC/.

Each cell in this table contains a structure. Each column of this table stands for a segment of the input except the first column, BOI, which corresponds to the "beginning of the input." Notice that each cell in the column headed i_1 contains a V; further, every structure in the column headed i_2 contains both a V and a C, in the correct order. The label on each row is a nonterminal of the position grammar, and corresponds to a type of syllable position. Notice that for each structure in the N row,

Table 8.1
DP table for /VC/ (structural descriptions only)

	BOI	$i_1 = V$	$i_2 = C$
S		⟨V⟩	⟨VC⟩
O	.□	.□V.□	.□V.C
N	.□□́	.□V	.□V.⟨C⟩
D	.□□́□.	.□V□.	.□VC.

Optimal Parse: .□V.⟨C⟩   This parse is represented in cell [N,i_2].

the last-generated (rightmost) position in the structure is a nucleus. The O row contains structures ending in an onset, while the D row contains structures ending in a coda. The S row only contains structures in which no positions at all have been generated (i.e., all the input segments seen are underparsed). Thus, each cell contains a structure that contains all the input segments up through the one heading the column of the cell, and with a last-generated syllable position corresponding to the row of the cell. The cell in row D and in column i_2, [D,i_2], contains a structure that includes the input segments i_1 and i_2, and the last-syllable position in the structure is a coda.

   The value of the table is that each cell does not contain just any structure meeting the requirements just described; each cell contains the best structure meeting those requirements. Each cell contains a structure representing the best way of parsing the input up through the segment for that column ending in the row-appropriate position. The last column (the column for the last input segment) includes the complete parses to be considered. The optimal parse is easily chosen from among this set of possibilities.

   In general, a given input string I is parsed by constructing a DP Table. The table has one column for each segment of the input, plus a first column, BOI. The BOI column is present because overparsed positions may be generated at the beginning, before any of the input has been examined (this would correspond to epenthesis at the beginning of the utterance). Each cell corresponds to a *partial description*, which is a structural description of part of the input. The table cell [N,i_2] corresponds to the optimal way of parsing up through the second segment of the input, with a nucleus being the last structural position in the partial description. Each cell also contains the constraint violation marks assessed the partial description, representing the Harmony of that partial description (these marks are not depicted in table 8.1).

The parsing algorithm proceeds by filling in the columns of the table one at a time, left to right. After the best way of parsing the input through segment i_{j-1} ending in each nonterminal has been calculated (the entries of column i_{j-1}), those values are then used to determine the best way (for each possible final position) of parsing the input through segment i_j (the entries of column i_j). Once all the values for the last column are determined, the Harmony values in the table cells of the last column in rows corresponding to possible finishing states are compared (this is explained in greater detail below). The cell (among those being compared) containing the highest Harmony value thus also contains the optimal parse of the input.

8.3.2 The Operations Set

Operations are used to fill cells in the DP Table. An operation works by taking the partial description in a previously filled cell, adding an element of structure to it, and putting the new description in the new cell. A cell entry is determined by considering all of the operations that might fill the cell, examining the partial descriptions created by each, and selecting the partial description with the highest resulting Harmony to actually fill the cell. This is the essence of dynamic programming: because the partial descriptions in later cells contain the partial descriptions listed in earlier cells, the earlier cell entries may be used directly, rather than explicitly recalculating all of the possibilities for later cells.

Each operation is based on one of three primitive actions.

(8.4)   The three primitive parsing actions
a. Parsing a segment of input into a new syllabic position
b. Underparsing an input segment
c. Overparsing a new syllabic position

Primitive actions (a) and (c) involve generating positions, so they must be coordinated with productions in the position grammar of *GEN*; (b) does not involve position generation. On the other hand, actions (a) and (b) consume input, while (c) does not. Operations are versions of the primitive actions coordinated with the specifics of the model (*GEN* and the universal constraints). An operation may be specified by four things: the new cell (being filled), the previous cell containing the description being added to, the structure added to the partial description, and the constraint violation marks incurred by the operation. A candidate structural description of an input may thus be viewed as resulting from a sequence of operations. It should be emphasized that an operation does not transform one entire structural description into another; it adds on to a partial description.

As an example, consider the actions that might fill cell $[O,i_2]$ of the DP Table. Recall that the structure in this cell must contain input segments i_1 and i_2, and the last syllabic position in the structure must be an onset. One possibility is the underparsing action: take the structure from the cell immediately to the left in the same row, $[O,i_1]$, and add to it the input segment i_2 marked as underparsed. We do not need to consider any other ways of filling this cell with i_2 underparsed, because we have already guaranteed that $[O,i_1]$ contains the best way of parsing through i_1 ending in an onset. The resulting Harmony of the operation will be the Harmony listed in $[O,i_1]$, with the mark {*PARSE} added to it (indicating the constraint violation resulting from the underparsing of i_2). If i_2 is a consonant, another possibility is to parse i_2 into a newly generated onset position. This requires having a structure from the previous column to which an onset position may be legally appended. The position grammar (8.1) shows that an onset position may be generated directly from the nonterminals S, N, and D; this corresponds to the intuitive notions that an onset must be at the beginning of a syllable, and may be the first position of a description (generated from S), may immediately follow a nucleus position (generated from N), or may immediately follow a coda position (generated from D). An onset position may not immediately follow another onset position, because then the first onset belongs to a syllable with no nucleus (recall that a syllable may not have more than one onset in CVT). Fortunately, we have already determined that the cells $[S,i_1]$, $[N,i_1]$, and $[D,i_1]$ contain the optimal partial descriptions for the allowed three cases. Finally, the cell $[O,i_2]$ may be filled by an overparsing operation that would take a structure which already contains i_2 and append an unfilled onset position.

The set of possible operations is called the *Operations Set* and is organized to indicate what operations may fill each type of cell (the cells are here typed by row). Table 8.2 shows the operations for filling cells in row

Table 8.2
The operations for filling an O row cell

New Cell	Condition	Previous Cell	Struc	Violations	Information	
					Production	Action Type
$[O,i_j]$		$[O,i_{j-1}]$	$\langle i_j \rangle$	{*PARSE}		Underparsing
$[O,i_j]$	IF i_j=C	$[S,i_{j-1}]$	o/i_j	{}	S → oO	Parsing
$[O,i_j]$	IF i_j=C	$[N,i_{j-1}]$	o/i_j	{}	N → oO	Parsing
$[O,i_j]$	IF i_j=C	$[D,i_{j-1}]$	o/i_j	{}	D → oO	Parsing
$[O,i_j]$		$[S,i_j]$	$o/\square$	{*FILL^{Ons}}	S → oO	Overparsing
$[O,i_j]$		$[N,i_j]$	$o/\square$	{*FILL^{Ons}}	N → oO	Overparsing
$[O,i_j]$		$[D,i_j]$	$o/\square$	{*FILL^{Ons}}	D → oO	Overparsing

O (the rest of the Operations Set for CVT appears in section 8.7). Each row in the table corresponds to an operation. The New Cell column shows the type of cell to be filled by the operation. The Condition column contains any additional conditions that must be met in order for the operation to apply (in this case, the restriction of V to nucleus positions, and so on). The Previous Cell column indicates the relative position of the cell containing the partial description being added to by the operation. The Struc column indicates the additional structure added by the operation. The Violations column shows the constraint violation marks incurred by the added structure. The final two columns are informational: the Production column lists the position grammar production used by the operation if one is used, and the Action Type column indicates the type of action. The term i_j in each operation is a variable, meant to match whatever segment heads the column of the cell currently being filled; the operations are the same for each column (input segment).

The Operations Set relates to the DP Table as follows. The Operations Set gives all of the possible operations that may fill a given cell in the DP Table. Each of the possible operations "competes" to fill in the cell. The product of each operation is a partial structure consisting of (a) the partial structure contained in the operation's previous cell with the operation's additional structure added to it, and (b) the Harmony of the new partial structure, which consists of the list of marks in the operation's previous cell with the marks incurred by the operation added to it. The operation producing the most harmonic partial description (that is, the one whose resulting list of marks is least offensive with respect to the constraint ranking of the grammar) actually gets to fill the cell. Told from the point of view of the algorithm, examine each of the operations that can fill the current cell, select the one that produces the most harmonic partial structural description, and place that operation's partial structural description and list of marks into the current cell.

The cell [S,BOI] is the starting cell: no input has yet been examined, and no positions have been generated. So, [S,BOI] has a Harmony value of no constraint violations in it. The other cells in the BOI column may be filled from there by overparsing operations. The cells in the BOI column may only be filled by overparsing operations, since there are no input segments for other operations to work with.

One crucial aspect has not yet been explained about the application of these operations. The parsing and underparsing operations have a previous state cell from the previous column in the DP Table, the column for segment i_{j-1}. However, the overparsing operations refer to other cells in the same column of the DP Table as the cell being filled. How, in general, can these cells be filled, if the value for each cell in the column depends on the values in the other cells of the column? The answer involves some intricate details of the algorithm and is given in the next section.

Notice that, in the Operations Table, the Parsing operations contain IF conditions. These are used to enforce constraints of CVT that consonants (C) may only fill onsets and codas, and vowels (V) only nuclei. These restrictions are assumed to be part of *GEN*, and so are included here as IF conditions, limiting the possible candidates.

8.3.3 Limiting Structure: Position Grammar Cycles

The overparsing operations consume no input, and so they map between cells within a single column. In principle, an unbounded number of such operations could apply, and in fact structures with arbitrary numbers of unfilled positions are specified by *GEN* (as formally defined). However, the algorithm need only explicitly consider a finite number of overparsing operations within a column. The position grammar has four nonterminals. Therefore, at most three overparsing operations can take place consecutively without the repeating of a nonterminal. A set of consecutive overparsings that both begins and ends with the same nonterminal can be considered a *cycle*. An example of a cycle of overparsings is an entire epenthesized syllable. The FILL constraints serve to penalize overparsing by penalizing any structural positions unfilled by input segments. One effect of these constraints is that cycles of overparsing operations are effectively banned (that is, no optimal structure will contain a cycle of overparsing).

This fact is not specific to CVT. For any theory within OT, the constraints must ban cycles of overparsings in order for the optimal value to be well defined. If the constraints make a description containing such a cycle more harmonic than a description differing only by the removal of that cycle, there is no optimal value, because one could always increase the Harmony by adding more such cycles of overparsings. If such cycles have no Harmony consequences, there will be an infinite number of optimal descriptions, because any optimal description can have more cycles of overparsings added to create a description with equal Harmony. Thus, for optimization with respect to the constraints to be well defined and reasonable, the constraints must strictly penalize overparsing cycles. The number of nonterminals in the position grammar bounds the number of consecutive overparsings that may occur without having a cycle.

Operations are properly applied to the DP Table by first filling in all cells of a column considering only underparsing and parsing operations (which only use values from the previous column). Next, a pass is then made through the column cells, considering the overparsing operations: if the resulting Harmony of an overparsing operation into a cell is higher than the Harmony already listed in the cell, replace the Harmony in the cell with that resulting from the considered overparsing operation. If at least one cell's entry was replaced by an overparsing operation, another pass is made through the column. This is repeated until a pass is made in which no overparsing operations replace any cell values. Because the constraints guarantee that cycles are not optimal, and there are four nonterminals in the position structure grammar of CVT, the maximum number of productive passes through a column is three.

The ban on overparsing cycles is the crucial observation that allows the algorithm to complete the search in a finite amount of time; although the space of structural descriptions to be searched is infinite, there is a provably correct (input-dependent) bound on the space of descriptions that actually need to be considered.

8.3.4 Selecting the Optimal Parse

Once the entire table has been completed, the optimal parse may be selected. In the position grammar, certain nonterminals may evaluate to the empty string. This means that they can be the last nonterminal in a derivation, and therefore that the syllable position to which each corresponds is a valid end of syllable position. Therefore, the cells in the final column, in rows corresponding to these nonterminals, contain valid complete parses of the input. For CVT, the nonterminals are N and D, signifying that a syllable may end in a nucleus or a coda, and S, for the null parse. These three entries are compared, and the entry with the highest Harmony is selected as the optimal parse of the input.

(8.5) The parsing algorithm
Note: OP(i_j) stands for the result (structure and marks) of applying operation OP to the appropriate cell in column i_j.
Parse(*Input* = i_1 thru i_n)
[S,BOI]:= no structure and no violation marks
repeat
    for each row X in BOI
        for each overparsing OP for X
            if ([X,BOI] < OP(BOI)) then [X,BOI] := OP(BOI)
        end-for
    end-for
until (no cell entries [X,BOI] change)

for each column i_j (j from 1 to n)
    for each row X
        [X,i_j] := the result of the underparsing OP for X
        for each parsing OP for X
            if ([X,i_j] < OP(i_j)) then [X,i_j] := OP(i_j)
        end-for
    end-for
    repeat
        for each row X
            for each overparsing OP for X
                if ([X,i_j] < OP(i_j)) then [X,i_j] := OP(i_j)
            end-for
        end-for

until (no cell entries change)
end-for
opt-cand := empty
for each row X that is a valid final position
   if (*opt-cand* < [X,i_n]) then *opt-cand* := [X,i_n]
end-for
return (*opt-cand*)

8.4   A Sample Parse

Table 8.3 shows the completed DP Table for the input /VC/, with the constraint ranking ONS ≫ NOCODA ≫ FILL^{Nuc} ≫ PARSE ≫ FILL^{Ons}.

The top line of each cell contains on the left an indication of the type of operation that filled the cell, and on the right (after the *from:* label) the row and column designation of the previous cell (the already-filled cell whose structure was added onto by the operation to fill the current cell). The abbreviations indicate the kind of operation that filled the cell: *over* for overparsing, *under* for underparsing, and *parse* for parsing. The constraint violation marks assessed the partial description are given on the middle line of each cell, and the bottom of each cell shows the partial

Table 8.3
The completed DP table for /VC/

	BOI	i_1 = V	i_2 = C
S	START	under from:[S,BOI] *PARSE ⟨V⟩	under from:[S,i_1] *PARSE *PARSE ⟨VC⟩
O	over from:[S,BOI] *FILL^{Ons} .□	over from:[N,i_1] *FILL^{Ons} *FILL^{Ons} .□V.□	parse from:[N,i_1] *FILL^{Ons} .□V.C
N	over from:[O,BOI] *FILL^{Ons} *FILL^{Nuc} .□◌́	parse from:[O,BOI] *FILL^{Ons} .□V	under from:[N,i_1] *FILL^{Ons} *PARSE .□V.⟨C⟩
D	over from:[N,BOI] *FILL^{Ons} *FILL^{Nuc} *NOCODA .□◌́□.	over from:[N,i_1] *FILL^{Ons} *NOCODA .□V□.	parse from:[N,i_1] *FILL^{Ons} *NOCODA .□VC.

Optimal Parse: .□V.⟨C⟩   This parse is represented in cell [N,i_2].

description contained by that cell. The cell containing the optimal parse is indicated manually, and the cells that constitute the steps in the construction of the optimal parse have heavy borders.

Parsing begins by filling the cells of the first column. The first cell, [S,BOI], is automatically filled with no structure, which incurs no constraint violations. Next, the cell [O,BOI] is filled. For this, the Operations Set is consulted. The Operations Set lists seven operations that can fill a cell in the O row (see Table 8.2). However, the underparsing and parsing operations do not apply here because they make reference to entries in an earlier column, which does not exist here. Of the three overparsing operations, two require entries in cells not yet filled: [N,BOI] and [D,BOI]. The remaining operation uses the entry in [S,BOI] as the previous cell and adds an unfilled onset position. This structure is placed in the cell, along with the incurred mark listed in the operation, $*\text{FILL}^{\text{Ons}}$. Next, the cell [N,BOI] is filled. Of the nine operations listed for a cell in the nucleus row, two may be considered here. The first is for previous cell [S,BOI], and results in violations of ONS and FILL^{Nuc}. The second is for previous cell [O,BOI], and results in violations of FILL^{Ons} and FILL^{Nuc}. Because $\text{ONS} \gg \text{FILL}^{\text{Ons}}$, the result of the first operation has lower Harmony than the result of the second; thus, the second operation gets to fill the cell. The cell [D,BOI] is filled similarly. That completes the first pass through the column for the overparsing operations. Next, a second pass is performed; now, for each cell, all of the overparsing operations may be considered, because each cell in the column contains an entry. However, no further overparsing operations change any of the cell entries, because none improve the Harmony of the entry, so the filling of the first column is complete after the second pass.

Now, column i_1 must be filled. The cells are first filled via the underparsing and parsing operations. We will focus in detail on how cell [O,i_1] gets filled. First, the one underparsing operation fills the cell; this results in a structure that has an unfilled onset position, and in which the first input segment, $i_1 = V$, is left unparsed. Next, the three parsing operations are considered. But none apply, because the input segment is a V, and an onset position may only have a C parsed into it. The underparsing and parsing operations for the rest of the column are now performed. The results of the steps up to this point are shown in table 8.4.

Table 8.4
The DP table with underparsing and parsing operations completed for column i_1

	BOI		$i_1 = V$		$i_2 = C$
S	START		under *Parse $\langle V \rangle$	[S,BOI]	
O	over *Fill^{Ons} .□	[S,BOI]	under *Fill^{Ons} *Parse .□$\langle V \rangle$	[O,BOI]	
N	over *Fill^{Ons} *Fill^{Nuc} .□□́	[O,BOI]	parse *Fill^{Ons} .□V	[O,BOI]	
D	over *Fill^{Ons} *Fill^{Nuc} *NoCoda .□□́□.	[N,BOI]	under *Fill^{Ons} *Fill^{Nuc} *NoCoda *Parse .□□́□.$\langle V \rangle$	[N,BOI]	

Finally, we consider the overparsing operations. For $[O,i_1]$, there are three overparsing operations, each of which appends an unfilled onset and incurs the mark *Fill^{Ons}. The first adds an unfilled onset to the structure in its previous cell, $[S,i_1]$, resulting in a partial structure with marks *Parse and *Fill^{Ons}. The second has previous cell $[N,i_1]$, and results in marks *Fill^{Ons} and *Fill^{Ons}. The third has previous cell $[D,i_1]$, and results in the marks *Fill^{Ons}, *Fill^{Nuc}, *NoCoda, *Parse, and *Fill^{Ons}. Of the three, the second overparsing operation has the highest resulting Harmony: the highest-ranked constraint violated by the second operation is Fill^{Ons}, while each of the other two violates a higher-ranked constraint. Importantly, it also has higher Harmony than the entry already in cell $[O,i_1]$, because Parse $\gg$ Fill^{Ons}. Therefore, the result of this overparsing operation replaces the earlier entry in the cell. Overparsing also replaces the entry in $[D,i_1]$. On the next pass through the column, no cell entries are replaced by further overparsing operations, so the column is complete.

Once all of the columns have been completed, the optimal parse may be selected. The final candidates are the structures in the cells in the final column, and in rows S, N, and D. Only these rows are considered because they correspond to the nonterminals that may evaluate to the empty string e in the position grammar (the possible final nonterminals). The optimal parse is in cell [N,i_2], as shown in table 8.3.

8.5   Interpretive Parsing

Basic interpretive parsing can be performed by the same type of algorithm as production-directed parsing (Tesar 1999). For interpretive parsing, the algorithm is applied to the overt form, with each segment of the overt form heading a column of the dynamic programing table. Importantly, the underparsing and overparsing operations are removed from the operating set (these nonfaithful operations are deactivated for the purposes of interpretive parsing). The consequence of this is that the candidate set is restricted to those candidates that exactly correspond to the overt form.

A more complex task is full interpretive parsing with a lexicon. This requires that the parser perform a morphological analysis of the overt form and produce a structural description that includes a correspondence relation between the elements of the overt form and individual lexical entries. Such a parser will necessarily be a part of any complete explanation of the learning of lexical underlying forms, and will be the subject of future research.

8.6   Discussion

8.6.1   Computational Complexity

Each column in the DP Table is processed in constant time for any fixed grammar: the number of cells in each column is the number of nonterminals in the position grammar, and the number of passes through the column is bounded from above by the number of nonterminals. There is one column for each input segment (plus the BOI column). Therefore, the algorithm is linear in the size of the input.

8.6.2   Ties

One possibility not shown in the above example is for two different operations to tie for optimality when attempting to fill a cell. To illustrate, there are two ways to derive an essentially identical partial description: first insert and then delete, or first delete and then insert. In this case, the tie might be seen as a kind of anomaly, having no significance to the ultimate phonetic realization. However, if more than one truly different partial description for the same cell incurred identical marks, including all of them in the cell permits all the optimal descriptions to be recovered from the table, if that cell should happen to figure in the set of descriptions ultimately found to be optimal.

8.6.3 Creating Parsers

For any given system with a regular position structure grammar, the Operations Set may be constructed as follows. First, for any cell $[X, i_j]$ where X is a nonterminal (x is the corresponding syllabic position unless X is S), one allowable operation is to underparse the input segment. So, include the underparsing operation that takes the structure in $[X, i_{j-1}]$ and adds an underparsed i_j to it. For each position grammar production with the nonterminal X on the right-hand side, two operations are possible: the generated position x has the next input segment parsed into it, or it is left overparsed. So, for each production $Y \Rightarrow xX$ generating X, create two operations: a parsing operation that takes the structure in $[Y, i_{j-1}]$ and appends a position x with i_j parsed into it, and an overparsing operation that takes the structure in $[Y, i_j]$ and appends an overparsed position x. Add to each operation any conditions that restrict its application (such as the restriction of vowels to nucleus positions in the Basic Syllable Theory). Finally, each operation must be supplied with marks indicating the constraint violations incurred by its application.

8.6.4 Regular and Context-Free Position Grammars

The fact that the position grammar used in the formal description of CVT is a regular grammar is very significant to guaranteeing the linear time efficiency of the parsing algorithm. However, the approach underlying the algorithm presented here may be extended to OT systems with context-free position structure grammars; the computational complexity is cubic in the general case. (See Tesar 1995, 1996 for further discussion and results.)

8.6.5 Locality

A property of CVT important to the success of the algorithm is the "locality" of the constraints. Each constraint may be evaluated on the basis of at most one input segment and two consecutive syllable positions. What really matters here is that the constraint violations

Table 8.5
The rest of the operations set

New Cell	Condition	Previous Cell	Struc	Violations	Information Production	Action Type
$[S, i_j]$		$[S,i_{j-1}]$	$\langle i_j \rangle$	{*PARSE}		Underparsing
$[N, i_j]$		$[N,i_{j-1}]$	$\langle i_j \rangle$	{*PARSE}		Underparsing
$[N, i_j]$	IF i_j=V	$[S,i_{j-1}]$	n/i_j	{*ONS}	S → nN	Parsing
$[N, i_j]$	IF i_j=V	$[O,i_{j-1}]$	n/i_j	{ }	O → nN	Parsing
$[N, i_j]$	IF i_j=V	$[N,i_{j-1}]$	n/i_j	{*ONS}	N → nN	Parsing
$[N, i_j]$	IF i_j=V	$[D,i_{j-1}]$	n/i_j	{*ONS}	D → nN	Parsing
$[N, i_j]$		$[S,i_j]$	$n/\square$	{*ONS *FILL^{Nuc}}	S → nN	Overparsing
$[N, i_j]$		$[O,i_j]$	$n/\square$	{*FILL^{Nuc}}	O → nN	Overparsing
$[N, i_j]$		$[N,i_j]$	$n/\square$	{*ONS *FILL^{Nuc}}	N → nN	Overparsing
$[N, i_j]$		$[D,i_j]$	$n/\square$	{*ONS *FILL^{Nuc}}	D → nN	Overparsing
$[D, i_j]$		$[D,i_{j-1}]$	$\langle i_j \rangle$	{*PARSE}		Underparsing
$[D, i_j]$	IF i_j=C	$[N,i_{j-1}]$	d/i_j	{*NoCODA}	N → dD	Parsing
$[D, i_j]$		$[N,i_j]$	$d/\square$	{*NoCODA}	N → dD	Overparsing

incurred by an operation can be determined solely on the basis of the operation itself. The information used by the constraints in CVT include the piece of structure added and the very end of the partial description being added on to (the last syllabic position generated). These restrictions on constraints are sufficient conditions for the dynamic programming approach. However, they are not necessary. Nonlocalities in constraint evaluation can be accommodated, if the possible interactions can be encapsulated into a finite number of information classes; see Tesar 1999 for discussion and examples of handling nonlocal constraints.

8.7   The Rest of the Operations Set

Table 8.5 provides the rest of the operations; the O row cell-filling operations were given in table 8.2.

Notes

Chapter 1

1. This assertion does not contradict Gold's (1978) theorem, which entails that, in the absence of negative data, certain infinite language families—such as the regular ("finite state"), the context-free, and families higher in the Chomsky hierarchy—are not learnable in the limit. To take an extreme example, consider languages over a single symbol a, writing in the obvious way $aa = a^2$, and so on. Then consider the following infinite family of infinite languages: $\mathcal{L} = \{L_1, L_2, L_3, \ldots\}$ where $L_1 = \{a, a^2, a^3, \ldots\}$, $L_2 = \{a^2, a^3, a^4, \ldots\}$, $L_3 = \{a^3, a^4, a^5, \ldots\}$, and so on. This family of languages $\mathcal{L}$ is so well structured that learnability in the limit is almost trivial. Consider the following algorithm. Let the learner's hypothesis after the ith learning datum be denoted H_i. Start with the hypothesis of the null language $H_0 = \emptyset$. When the ith learning datum a^k is observed, hypothesize the language $H_i \equiv H_{i-1} \cup \{a^k, a^{k+1}, a^{k+2}, \ldots\}$—that is, the language $\{a^m, a^{m+1}, a^{m+2}, \ldots\} = L_m$ where m is the smallest "power" of a (i.e., string length) yet observed. Now suppose the target language is L_t. Then eventually the smallest power admitted by the language (a^t) will be observed, and from this point on the algorithm will always hypothesize the correct language L_t. As this simple example shows, *size* does not matter: it is the *structure* of the space of possible languages that is really critical.

2. By *neural network* we will mean a collection of interconnected processing elements, each carrying an "activation value" that influences that of connected elements via connections with differing numerical strengths. These strengths or weights are the parameters that distinguish different networks and determine which function they will compute, as they convert input activity (perhaps encoding the radar image of a submarine) into output activity (perhaps encoding a classification of the image as a certain type of submarine).

3. This is the case even when triggering forms exist for all parameter settings, and those forms appear among those presented to the learner with some reasonable frequency.

4. Any algorithm is a solution to an abstract, formal problem, and thus to any particular problem that can be cast as an instance of that formal problem. Thus our learning algorithms apply to any learning problem in which the learner's task is to find an unknown ranking of a given set of constraints with respect to which a given set of structures are optimal. Because the only known problem with this structure is that of learning grammars under OT, this algorithm can be said to exploit structure that is distinctly linguistic in character. By contrast, generic P&P learning algorithms apply to any learning problem in which the search space is parameterized; this weak structure is shared by a huge class of learning problems, in which parameterized grammars have no distinguished status. Thus the weak generic P&P learning algorithms are equally suitable a priori to Chomskian P&P grammar learning, to OT grammar learning, to learning to distinguish rocks from submarines by their sonar echoes, and to a host of other problems. The algorithms developed below acquire their relative strength from exploiting stronger structure characteristic of a much more restricted class of learning problems: only of the OT grammar learning problem, as far as we know.

5. This characterization corresponds most closely to the Viterbi algorithm; see, for example, Nádas and Mercer 1996, Smolensky 1996c.

6. Readers well versed in the theory of EM algorithms will notice that this formulation of iterative learning algorithms differs from classical EM algorithms in the way hidden structure is selected *for learning* in step 1. Classical EM algorithms assign, as the value of hidden structure, the *expected value*, or average value, of the hidden structure, given a particular model (hence the *Expectation* in Expectation Maximization). This is true despite the fact that, once learning is complete, the model will typically be used to assign, as the value of hidden structure, the value optimizing the probability of the resulting paired overt/hidden structure.

We have chosen to characterize iterative learning approaches in terms of selecting the *optimal value* of hidden structure, rather than the expected value of hidden structure, for several reasons. In the types of problems to which EM algorithms are typically applied, models are defined in terms of probability, and expected values are usually unproblematic to define. Not so the nonprobabilistic Harmony functions used in OT. In fact, selecting the optimal value of hidden structure can be viewed as the concept of expected value most faithful to the "winner-take-all" spirit of OT. Further, by having the learning algorithm use the optimal value of hidden structure, greater parsimony is achieved between learning and general psycholinguistic processing: the interpretation process used for learning is identical to the interpretation process used for language comprehension generally. This decision to have step 1 use optimal values for hidden structure, rather than average values, does have real consequences for algorithm behavior. These consequences are exemplified and discussed in detail in chapter 4.

7. The probability p of a representation x is exponentially related to its Harmony H: $p(x) \propto e^{H(x)}$.

Chapter 2

1. The set *Con* of constraints is universal: the same constraints are present in all languages. The simplest interpretation of this is that the constraints are innately specified, but that is not required by the theory itself: OT only requires that *Con* be universal. Neither the authors nor their research programs are committed to the innateness of *Con*; however, all the work in this book presumes that the constraints in *Con* are available to the learner as early as could possibly be useful. Obviously, any alternative theory would have to say more about how the constraints are developed, as well as how universality is to be maintained.

An OT-based acquisition theory in which significant components of *Con* are learned would likely require methods like those developed here for analyzing the part of the learning problem requiring that constraints—irrespective of their source—be correctly ranked for the target language. Such a theory would also likely require methods like those developed here for solving the problem of jointly learning the grammar and the hidden structure in learning data.

So while the work presented here does not address learning of constraints, the contributions are nonetheless likely to inform any ultimate theory of OT grammar learning, irrespective of the degree to which *Con* is innate.

2. *ONSET* and *NOCODA* are the more readable names from McCarthy and Prince 1993 for the constraints P&S call *ONS* and *-COD*.

3. These constraints constitute the parse/fill model of faithfulness in OT. The parse/fill model is used in P&S and in much of the OT literature. More recently, an alternative conception of faithfulness has been proposed, the correspondence model (McCarthy and Prince 1995). The distinctions between the two are irrelevant to the learnability work described in this book; the same results hold for OT grammars adopting the correspondence model of faithfulness.

4. Determining that this candidate is optimal requires demonstrating that it is more harmonic than *any* of the infinitely many competing candidates; see the discussion below, and chapter 2, note 5.

5. This can be briefly illustrated in reference to optimal candidate (d) of table 2.1. Here, avoiding the mark *PARSE of (d) entails violating either higher-ranked NOCODA (as in candidate (a)) or higher-ranked FILL^{Nuc} (as in candidate (c)), and avoiding the mark *FILL^{Ons} of (d) entails violating either ONSET (as in (a)) or PARSE (as in (b)); both of these constraints are higher ranked than FILL^{Ons}. This proves that candidate (d) is more harmonic than all the infinitely many other candidates in *Gen(/VCVC/)*.

Chapter 3

1. There are N choices for I, and for each one, $N - 1$ choices for a different j. This gives $N \times (N - 1)$ ordered pairs. This counts each pair of constraints twice, as (j,i) and (i,j), so dividing by 2 we get the number of *unordered* pairs, $N(N - 1)/2$.

2. There are subtleties here that require considerable caution. There is not a one-to-one correspondence between the demotions arising from informative examples and the setting of the ranking parameters. For example, a constraint $\mathbb{C}_i$ may be demoted below another $\mathbb{C}_j$ at one point during learning, and then $\mathbb{C}_j$ may be demoted below $\mathbb{C}_i$ later. Thus the ij ranking parameter would be set one way first, then the other way later. Given this, it is unclear why the number of informative examples needed cannot be greater than the number of parameters, or, indeed, why Constraint Demotion is ever guaranteed to converge to a solution. The ranking parameters may not be an effective formal tool in analyzing the algorithm, although they are conceptually helpful in understanding how the ranking structure on the space of grammars can enable efficient search through an enormous space. The technically more powerful analytic tool is the concept of h-domination, developed in chapter 7.

3. There is a choice to be made in exactly how to apply EDCD to a set of observed, optimal structural descriptions, resulting in two variations. Because applying CD to a single mark-data pair does not ensure that the observed parse (the winner) is yet optimal with respect to *all* candidates (not just the loser), the learner could re-parse the same input according to the new constraint ranking. If the resulting parse is different from the winner, the new parse may be used to create a new mark-data pair, to which CD is applied. This process could be repeated until the learner's hierarchy selects the winner as the optimal description. This allows the learner to extract more information out of a single winner, at the cost of greater processing dedicated to each winner. The decision here is whether or not to repeatedly apply parsing and CD to a single winner.

Chapter 5

1. Future OT work on syntax is likely to take on syntactic properties of lexical items, such as argument structure, where related acquisition issues may be expected to arise.

2. The formulation of P&S is slightly different: only underlying forms that *optimally* surface as ϕ are considered. In our version, *all* structures that surface as ϕ are considered, because we want to use lexicon optimization as part of a learning process; when the current grammar is incorrect, there may well be no underlying forms that optimally surface as ϕ. Thus our formulation of lexicon optimization is "robust" in the same sense as our formulation of interpretive parsing: even when there is no grammatical option, the maximal-Harmony (but ungrammatical) structure is used nonetheless.

3. Lexicon optimization is easily extended to handle paradigms with alternating morphemes, despite claims to the contrary (Hale and Reiss 1998, p. 667). Our formulation is quite similar to the one adopted in Inkelas (1994, pp. 6–7), the very paper that Hale and Reiss incorrectly cite as arguing against lexicon optimization with alternations. In fact, a main point of (the paper by Inkelas 1994) is to show that lexicon optimization applies quite effectively to alternations, permitting a much more restricted use of underspecification.

4. We have simplified slightly here; Lombardi's actual constraints are as follows. IDONSLAR requires that an output consonant preceding a tautosyllabic sonorant/vowel agree in Larnygeal features with its corresponding input segment (ONSFAITH); LAR penalizes Laryngeal features (VOI); and MALAR requires any Laryngeal features in the input to appear in its corresponding output segment (FAITH). Output-output faithfulness constraints (OO-FAITH) do not figure in her analysis.

5. See also the lexicon optimization "tableaux des tableaux" of Itô, Mester, and Padgett 1995.

6. This point reveals a fundamental flaw in the parsing proposal of Hale and Reiss (1998): their parser performs no *morphological analysis* of overt forms into multiple morphemes. Since alternations only arise when a single morpheme is identified as surfacing differently in different contexts, morphological analysis must be part of parsing in any account wishing to directly address issues of alternation. Further, even in the case of monomorphemic words, it is much more sensible for a parser to actively employ the lexicon while parsing the word, rather than enumerating a (possibly infinite) list of all possible underlying forms and only later consulting the lexicon.

7. In this context it is clear why the version of lexicon optimization needed must allow for situations in which no outputs optimal for the currently hypothesized, incorrect, grammar have the correct overt form (see chapter 5, note 2). If the current grammar were not a coda-devoicing grammar (or an intervocalic voicing grammar), no underlying form for "day" would produce the correct surface paradigm. As formulated here, lexicon optimization considers all outputs with the correct overt form, even if they are not optimal. Thus, outputs like those in table 5.2 would still be considered, and some underlying form for "day" would be hypothesized: the one yielding the maximum-Harmony output paradigm given the currently hypothesized grammar. If the choice is /tag/, subsequent learning steps will rerank constraints to produce a coda-devoicing grammar.

Chapter 6

1. Under the normal definitions of *trigger*, a single datum can be a trigger for more than one parameter, but is such independently. In such a case, the datum would not be interpreted as expressing any relationship between the values of the two parameters.

References

Ackema, Peter, and Ad Neeleman. 1998. Optimal questions. In *Is the best good enough? Optimality and competition in syntax*, ed. Pilar Barbosa, Danny Fox, Paul Hagstrom, Martha McGinnis, and David Pesetsky, 15–33. Cambridge, MA: MIT Press and *MIT Working Papers in Linguistics*. ROA-69.

Angluin, Dana. 1978. Inductive inference of formal languages from positive data. *Information and Control* 45:117–135.

Bahl, Lalit R., Fredrick Jelinek, and Robert L. Mercer. 1983. A maximum likelihood approach to continuous speech recognition. *IEEE Transactions on Pattern Analysis and Machine Intelligence* PAMI-5, 179–190.

Barbosa, Pilar, Danny Fox, Paul Hagstrom, Martha McGinnis, and David Pesetsky, eds. 1998. *Is the best good enough? Optimality and competition in syntax*. Cambridge, MA: MIT Press and *MIT Working Papers in Linguistics*.

Baum, L. E., and T. Petrie. 1966. Statistical inference for probabilistic functions of finite state Markov chains. *Annals of Mathematical Statistics* 37:1559–1563.

Benua, Laura. 1995. Identity effects in morphological truncation. In *University of Massachusetts Occasional Papers in Linguistics* 18: *Papers in Optimality Theory*, ed. J. Beckman, L. W. Dickey, and S. Urbanczyk, 77–136. GLSA, University of Massachusetts, Amherst. ROA-74.

Berwick, Robert. 1986. *The acquisition of syntactic knowledge*. Cambridge, MA: MIT Press.

Billings, Loren, and Catherine Rudin. 1994. Optimality and superiority: A new approach to overt multiple *wh*-ordering. In *Annual Workshop on Formal Approaches to Slavic Linguistics: The College Park Meeting, 1994*, ed. Jindrich Toman, 35–60. Ann Arbor: Michigan Slavic Publications.

Brown, Peter F., John Cocke, Stephen A. Della Pietra, Vincent J. Della Pietra, Fredrick Jelinek, John D. Lafferty, Robert L. Mercer, and Paul S. Roossin. 1990. A statistical approach to machine translation. *Computational Linguistics* 16:79–85.

Buckley, Eugene. 1995. Cyclicity as correspondence. Paper presented at the University of Maryland, Nov. 10. ROA-93c.

Burzio, Luigi. 1993. English stress, vowel length, and modularity. *Journal of Linguistics* 29:359–418.

Burzio, Luigi. 1994. *Principles of English stress*. Cambridge, England: Cambridge University Press.

Burzio, Luigi. 1995. The rise of Optimality Theory. *Glot International* 1(6):3–7.

Burzio, Luigi. 1998. Multiple correspondence. *Lingua* 104(1–2):79–109.

Burzio, Luigi. To appear. Surface constraints vs. underlying representations. In *Current trends in phonology: Models and methods*, ed. Jacques Durand and Bernard Laks. CNRS, Paris X, and University of Salford Publications.

Charniak, Eugene. 1993. *Statistical language learning*. Cambridge, MA: MIT Press.

Chomsky, Noam. 1981. *Lectures on government and binding*. Dordrecht: Foris.

Clark, Eve. 1987. The principle of contrast: A constraint on language acquisition. In *Mechanisms of language acquisition*, ed. Brian MacWhinney, 1–33. Hillsdale, NJ: Erlbaum.

Clark, Robin. 1990. Papers on learnability and natural selection. Technical reports in formal and computational linguistics, no. 1, Université de Genève.

Clements, George N., and Samuel Jay Keyser. 1983. *CV phonology*. Cambridge, MA: MIT Press.

Corman, Thomas, Charles Leiserson, and Ronald Rivest. 1990. *Introduction to algorithms*. Cambridge, MA: MIT Press.

Daelemans, Walter, Steven Gillis, and Gert Durieux. 1994. The acquisition of stress: A data-oriented approach. *Computational Linguistics* 20:421–451.

Dempster, A. P., N. M. Laird, and D. B. Rubin. 1977. Maximum likelihood estimation from incomplete data via the EM algorithm. *Journal of the Royal Statistical Society B* 39:1–38.

Demuth, Katherine. 1995. Markedness and the development of prosodic structure. In *NELS 25*, 13–25. GLSA, University of Massachusetts, Amherst. ROA-50.

Dresher, B. Elan. 1999. Charting the learning path: Cues to parameter setting. *Linguistic Inquiry* 30:27–67.

Dresher, B. Elan, and Jonathan Kaye. 1990. A computational learning model for metrical phonology. *Cognition* 34:137–195.

Eisner, Jason. 1997. Efficient generation in primitive Optimality Theory. In *Proceedings of the 35th Annual Meeting of the Association for Computational Linguistics*. San Francisco: Morgan Kaufmann. ROA-206.

Ellison, T. Mark. 1994. Phonological derivation in Optimality Theory. In *Proceedings of the 15th International Conference on Computational Linguistics*, 1007–1013. ROA-75.

Flemming, Edward, and Michael Kenstowicz. 1995. Base-identity and uniform exponence: Alternatives to cyclicity. Ms., Linguistics Department, MIT.

Frank, Robert, and Shyam Kapur. 1996. On the use of triggers in parameter setting. *Linguistic Inquiry* 27:623–660.

Frank, Robert, and Giorgio Satta. 1998. Optimality Theory and the generative complexity of constraint violability. *Computational Linguistics* 24:307–315.

Furby, Christine. 1974. Garawa phonology. *Papers in Australian Linguistics* 7:1–11.

Gafos, Adamantios. 1996. On the notion "paradigm structure" in Temiar. Paper presented at the GLOW '96 workshop on the morphology-phonology interface.

Gibson, Edward, and Ken Wexler. 1994. Triggers. *Linguistic Inquiry* 24:407–454.

Gnanadesikan, Amalia. 1995. Markedness and faithfulness constraints in child phonology. Ms., Linguistics Department, University of Massachusetts. ROA-67.

Gold, E. M. 1978. Complexity of automatic identification from given data. *Information and Control* 37:302–320.

Grimshaw, Jane. 1990. *Argument Structure*. Cambridge, MA: MIT Press.

Grimshaw, Jane. 1993. Minimal projection, heads, and inversion. Ms., Linguistics Department, Rutgers University, New Brunswick, NJ. (Revision: ROA-68.)

Grimshaw, Jane. 1997. Projection, heads, and optimality. *Linguistic Inquiry* 28:373–422.

Grimshaw, Jane, and Vieri Samek-Lodovici. 1995. Optimal subjects. In *University of Massachusetts Occasional Papers in Linguistics* 18: *Papers in Optimality Theory*, ed. J. Beckman, L. W. Dickey, and S. Urbanczyk, 589–605. GLSA, University of Massachusetts, Amherst.

Grimshaw, Jane, and Vieri Samek-Lodovici. 1998. Optimal subjects and subject universals. In *Is the best good enough? Optimality and competition in syntax*, ed. Pilar Barbosa, Danny Fox, Paul Hagstrom, Martha McGinnis, and David Pesetsky, 193–219. Cambridge, MA: MIT Press and *MIT Working Papers in Linguistics*.

Gupta, Prahlad, and David Touretzky. 1994. Connectionist models and linguistic theory: Investigations of stress systems in language. *Cognitive Science* 18:1–50.

Hale, Mark, and Charles Reiss. 1998. Formal and empirical arguments concerning phonological acquisition. *Linguistic Inquiry* 29(4):656–683.

Hamburger, Henry, and Ken Wexler. 1973. Identifiability of a class of transformational grammars. In *Approaches to natural language*, ed. Jaakko Hintikka, J. M. E. Moravcsik, and Patrick Suppes. Dordrecht: Reidel.

Hammond, Michael. 1990a. Deriving ternarity. Ms., Linguistics Department, University of Arizona, Tucson.

Hammond, Michael. 1990b. Metrical theory and learnability. Ms., Linguistics Department, University of Arizona, Tucson.

Hammond, Michael. 1995. Syllable parsing in French and English. Ms., Linguistics Department, University of Arizona, Tucson.

Hammond, Michael. 1997. Parsing in OT. Ms., Linguistics Department, University of Arizona, Tucson. ROA-222.

Haussler, David. 1996. Probably Approximately Correct learning and decision-theoretic generalizations. In *Mathematical perspectives on neural networks*, ed. Paul Smolensky, Michael C. Mozer, and David E. Rumelhart, 651–718. Hillsdale, NJ: Erlbaum.

Hayes, Bruce. 1980. A metrical theory of stress rules. Doctoral dissertation, Linguistics Department, MIT.

Hayes, Bruce. 1995. *Metrical stress theory: Principles and case studies*. Chicago: University of Chicago Press.

Hinton, Geoffrey. 1989. Connectionist learning procedures. *Artificial Intelligence* 40: 185–234.

Inkelas, Sharon. 1994. The consequences of optimization for underspecification. Ms., Linguistics Department, University of California, Berkeley, October. ROA-40.

Itô, Junko, R. Armin Mester, and Jaye Padgett. 1995. Licensing and underspecification in Optimality Theory. *Linguistic Inquiry* 26:571–613.

Jakobson, Roman. 1962. *Selected writings 1: Phonological studies*. The Hague: Mouton.

Kager, René. 1994. Ternary rhythm in alignment theory. Ms., Research Institute for Language and Speech. Utrecht University. ROA-35.

Karttunen, Lauri. 1998. The proper treatment of optimality in computational phonology. Ms., Xerox Research Centre Europe. ROA-258.

Kay, Martin. 1980. Algorithmic schemata and data structures in syntactic parsing. CSL-80-12, October.

Kearns, Michael, and Umesh Vazirani. 1994. *An introduction to computational learning theory*. Cambridge, MA: MIT Press.

Kenstowicz, Michael. 1995a. Base-identity and uniform exponence: Alternatives to cyclicity. Ms., Linguistics Department, MIT. ROA-105.

Kenstowicz, Michael. 1995b. Cyclic vs. non-cyclic constraint evaluation. *Phonology* 12:397–436. ROA-31.

Legendre, Géraldine, Yoshiro Miyata, and Paul Smolensky. 1990a. Can connectionism contribute to syntax? Harmonic Grammar, with an application. *Proceedings of the 26th Annual Meeting of the Chicago Linguistic Society*. Chicago.

Legendre, Géraldine, Yoshiro Miyata, and Paul Smolensky. 1990b. Harmonic Grammar— A formal multi-level connectionist theory of linguistic well-formedness: Theoretical foundations. *Proceedings of the 12th Annual Conference of the Cognitive Science Society*, 388–395. Hillsdale, NJ: Erlbaum.

Legendre, Géraldine, William Raymond, and Paul Smolensky. 1993. Analytic typology of case marking and grammatical voice. *Proceedings of the 19th Annual Meeting of the Berkeley Linguistics Society*, 464–478. Berkeley Linguistics Society, University of California, Berkeley. ROA-3.

Legendre, Géraldine, Paul Smolensky, and Colin Wilson. 1998. When is less more? Faithfulness and minimal links in *wh*-chains. In *Is the best good enough? Optimality and competition in syntax*, ed. Pilar Barbosa, Danny Fox, Paul Hagstrom, Martha McGinnis, and David Pesetsky, 249–289. Cambridge, Mass: MIT Press and *MIT Working Papers in Linguistics*. ROA-117.

Legendre, Géraldine, Colin Wilson, Paul Smolensky, Kristin Homer, and William Raymond. 1995. Optimality and *wh*-extraction. In *University of Massachusetts Occasional Papers in Linguistics* 18: *Papers in Optimality Theory*, ed. J. Beckman, L. W. Dickey, and S. Urbanczyk, 607–636. GLSA, University of Massachusetts, Amherst. ROA-85.

Levelt, Clara. 1995. Unfaithful kids: Place of Articulation patterns in early child language. Paper presented at the Department of Cognitive Science, Johns Hopkins University, Baltimore, September.

Liberman, Mark, and Alan Prince. 1977. On stress and linguistic rhythm. *Linguistic Inquiry* 8:249–336.

Lombardi, L. 1995. Positional faithfulness and the phonology of voicing in Optimality Theory. Ms., Linguistics Department, University of Maryland.

McCarthy, John. 1995. Extensions of faithfulness: Rotuman revisited. Ms., Linguistics Department, University of Massachusetts. ROA-64.

McCarthy, John, and Alan Prince. 1993. Prosodic Morphology I: constraint interaction and satisfaction. Ms., Linguistics Department, University of Massachusetts, Amherst, and Linguistics Department, Rutgers University, New Brunswick, NJ. (To appear, MIT Press.)

McCarthy, John, and Alan Prince. 1995. Faithfulness and reduplicative identity. In *University of Massachusetts Occasional Papers in Linguistics* 18: *Papers in Optimality Theory*, eds. J. Beckman, L. W. Dickey, and S. Urbanczyk, 249–384. GLSA, University of Massachusetts, Amherst. ROA-60.

Nádas, Arthur, and Robert L. Mercer. 1996. Hidden Markov models and some connections with artificial neural nets. In *Mathematical perspectives on neural networks*, ed. Paul Smolensky, Michael C. Mozer, and David E. Rumelhart, 603–650. Hillsdale, NJ: Erlbaum.

Niyogi, Partha, and Robert C. Berwick. 1996. A language learning model for finite parameter spaces. In *Computational approaches to language acquisition*, ed. Michael R. Brent, 161–193. Cambridge, MA: MIT Press.

Pater, Joe, and Johanne Paradis. 1996. Truncation without templates in child phonology. In *Proceedings of the 20th Annual Boston University Conference on Language Development*, 540–552. Somerville, MA: Cascadilla Press.

Pinker, Steven. 1986. Productivity and conservatism in language acquisition. In *Language learning and concept acquisition*, ed. William Demopoulos and Ausonio Marras, 54–79. Norwood, NJ: Ablex.

Pitt, Leonard, and Leslie Valiant 1988. Computational limitations on learning from examples. *Journal of the ACM* 35:965–984.

Prince, Alan. 1990. Quantitative consequences of rhythmic organization. In *CLS26-II: Papers from the Parasession on the Syllable in Phonetics and Phonology*, ed. K. Deaton, M. Noske, and M. Ziolkowski, 355–398.

Prince, Alan, and Paul Smolensky. 1991. Notes on connectionism and Harmony Theory in linguistics. Technical Report CU-CS-533-91. Department of Computer Science, University of Colorado, Boulder.

Prince, Alan, and Paul Smolensky. 1993. Optimality Theory: Constraint interaction in generative grammar. Ms., Rutgers University, New Brunswick, NJ, and University of Colorado, Boulder. Technical Report RuCCS TR-2. Rutgers Center for Cognitive Science. (To appear, MIT Press.)

Pulleyblank, Douglas, and William J. Turkel. 1995. Traps in constraint ranking space. Paper presented at Maryland Mayfest 95: Formal Approaches to Learnability, University of Maryland, College Park.

Pulleyblank, Douglas, and William J. Turkel. 1998. The logical problem of language acquisition in Optimality Theory. In *Is the best good enough? Optimality and competition in syntax*, ed. Pilar Barbosa, Danny Fox, Paul Hagstrom, Martha McGinnis, and David Pesetsky, 399–420. Cambridge, MA: MIT Press and *MIT Working Papers in Linguistics*.

Rabiner, L. R. 1989. A Tutorial on hidden Markov models and selected applications in speech recognition. *Proceedings of the IEEE* 77(2):257–286.

Safir, Ken. 1987. Comments on Wexler and Manzini. In *Parameter setting*, ed. Thomas Roeper and Edwin Williams, 77–89. Dordrecht: Reidel.

Samek-Lodovici, Vieri. 1994. Structural focusing and subject inversion in Italian. Ms., Rutgers University, New Brunswick, NJ.

Samek-Lodovici, Vieri. 1996. Constraints on subjects: An Optimality Theoretic analysis. Doctoral dissertation, Department of Linguistics, Rutgers University, New Brunswick, NJ.

Sankoff, David, and Joseph Kruskal. 1983. *Time warps, string edits, and macromolecules: The theory and practice of sequence comparison.* Reading, MA: Addison-Wesley.

Smolensky, Paul. 1983. Schema selection and stochastic inference in modular environments. *Proceedings of the National Conference on Artificial Intelligence*, 378–382.

Smolensky, Paul. 1986. Information processing in dynamical systems: Foundations of Harmony Theory. In *Parallel distributed processing: Explorations in the microstructure of cognition. Volume 1: Foundations*, ed. David Rumelhart, James McClelland, and the PDP Research Group, 194–281. Cambridge, MA: MIT Press/Bradford Books.

Smolensky, Paul. 1996a. On the comprehension/production dilemma in child language. *Linguistic Inquiry* 27:720–731. ROA-118.

Smolensky, Paul. 1996b. The initial state and "richness of the base" in Optimality Theory. Technical report JHU-CogSci-96-4. Department of Cognitive Science, Johns Hopkins University, Baltimore.

Smolensky, Paul. 1996c. Statistical perspectives on neural networks. In *Mathematical perspectives on neural networks*, ed. Paul Smolensky, Michael C. Mozer, and David E. Rumelhart, 453–495. Hillsdale, NJ: Erlbaum.

Tesar, Bruce. 1994. Parsing in Optimality Theory: A dynamic programming approach. Technical Report CU-CS-714-94. Department of Computer Science, University of Colorado, Boulder.

Tesar, Bruce. 1995. Computational Optimality Theory. Doctoral dissertation, Department of Computer Science, University of Colorado, Boulder. ROA-90.

Tesar, Bruce. 1996. Computing optimal descriptions for Optimality Theory grammars with context-free position structures. In *Proceedings of the 34th Annual Meeting of the Association for Computational Linguistics*, 101–107. San Francisco: Morgan Kaufmann.

Tesar, Bruce. 1997. An iterative strategy for learning metrical stress in Optimality Theory. In *Proceedings of the 21st Annual Boston University Conference on Language Development*, ed. Elizabeth Hughes, Mary Hughes, and Annabel Greenhill, 615–626. Somerville, MA: Cascadilla Press.

Tesar, Bruce. 1998a. Error-driven learning in Optimality Theory via the efficient computation of optimal forms. In *Is the best good enough? Optimality and competition in syntax*, ed. Pilar Barbosa, Danny Fox, Paul Hagstrom, Martha McGinnis, and David Pesetsky, 421–435. Cambridge, MA: MIT Press and *MIT Working Papers in Linguistics*.

Tesar, Bruce. 1998b. An iterative strategy for language learning. *Lingua* 104:131–145.

Tesar, Bruce. 1998c. Using the mutual inconsistency of structural descriptions to overcome ambiguity in language learning. In *Proceedings of the North East Linguistic Society 28*, ed. Pius N. Tamanji and Kiyomi Kusumoto, 469–483. GLSA, University of Massachusetts, Amherst.

Tesar, Bruce. 1999. Robust interpretive parsing in metrical stress theory. In *Proceedings of the 17th West Coast Conference on Formal Linguistics*, ed. Kimary Shahin, Susan Blake, and Eun-Sook Kim, 625–639. Stanford, CA: CSLI Publications. [Distributed by Cambridge University Press.]

Tesar, Bruce, and Paul Smolensky. 1993. The learnability of Optimality Theory: An algorithm and some basic complexity results. Technical Report CU-CS-678-93. Department of Computer Science, University of Colorado, Boulder. ROA-2.

Tesar, Bruce, and Paul Smolensky. 1995. The learnability of Optimality Theory. In *Proceedings of the 13th West Coast Conference on Formal Linguistics*, ed. Raul Aranovich, William Byrne, Susanne Preuss, and Martha Senturia, 122–137. Stanford, CA: CSLI Publications. [Distributed by Cambridge University Press.]

Tesar, Bruce, and Paul Smolensky. 1996. Learnability in Optimality Theory (long version). Technical Report JHU-CogSci-96-4. Department of Cognitive Science, Johns Hopkins University, Baltimore.

Tesar, Bruce, and Paul Smolensky. 1998. Learnability in Optimality Theory. *Linguistic Inquiry* 29:229–268.

Wexler, Kenneth. 1981. Some issues in the theory of learnability. In *The logical problem of language acquisition*, ed. C. L. Baker and John McCarthy, 30–52. Cambridge, MA: MIT Press.

Wexler, Kenneth, and Peter Culicover. 1980. *Formal principles of language acquisition*. Cambridge, MA: MIT Press.

Wexler, Kenneth, and M. Rita Manzini. 1987. Parameters and learnability in binding theory. In *Parameter setting*, ed. Thomas Roeper and Edwin Williams, 41–76. Dordrecht: Reidel.

Index

Acquisition. *See* Language acquisition
Antiallomorphy, 78

Basic CV Syllable Theory (CVT), 19
  and Constraint Demotion, 38–41
  formalizing, 113–114
  parsing, 115–123
  and Recursive Constraint Demotion,
    101–106

Comprehension, language, 13
Computational Learning Theory, 48
Con, 21
Constraints
  alignment, 55
  for CVT, 22
  for GSL, 22–23
  for stress, 54
Constraint Demotion. *See also* Robust
  Interpretive Parsing / Constraint
  Demotion; Recursive Constraint
  Demotion
  correctness of, 43, 46
  data complexity of, 44, 46, 100
  error-driven. *See* Error-Driven Constraint
    Demotion
  principle of, 36
  procedure, 95
  recursive. *See* Recursive Constraint
    Demotion
Contrast (Principle of), 48
Cue learning, 3, 4, 73
CVT. *See* Basic CV Syllable Theory
Cycle of overparsings. *See* Overparsing
  cycle

Disjunctions (in learning), 42–43
Dynamic programming, 111–113, 115
Dynamic Programming (DP) Table,
  115–117

Error-Driven Constraint Demotion, 50–52,
  99–100
Error-driven learning, 52
  with Recursive Constraint Demotion, 110
Expectation Maximization (EM)
  algorithm, 9

Faithfulness
  constraints, 22, 75, 78
  output/output, 78
  and parsing. *See* Parsing, production-
    directed
Fatal violation. *See* Mark, fatal

Garawa, 53–54, 56
Gen, 20
  parsing with, 113
Generation, language, 13
Genetic algorithms, 6
GSL, 19

H-distance, 96
H-domination, 92
Harmonic bounding, 65
Harmonic Grammar, 11
Harmonic ordering, 24, 26
  and stratified hierarchies, 37–38
Harmony, 24
  at the paradigm level, 78–80
Harmony Theory, 10–11
Hidden Markov models, 8, 115
Hierarchy, 24
  initial, 38–39, 46–47, 69–71, 75–76, 97–99
  stratified, 37, 47–48, 91
  target, 92
  totally ranked, 37, 47–50, 91

Implicit negative evidence, 33, 86
Independence (of parameters), 85
Informative pair, 44, 96
Interpretation, 57
Iterative algorithms, 8–12, 82

Language acquisition
  child data, 76
  decomposition of the problem, 6–7, 80–83
  the logical problem of, 2
  statistical approaches, 72
Language interpretation, 57
Language production, 57
Lexicon optimization, 77–78
  paradigm-level, 79
Locality, 127–128
Loser/winner pair, 35

Mark
  canceled and uncanceled, 25
  constraint violation, 21
  fatal, 38, 40
Mark Cancelation, 25, 28, 94–95
  and stratified hierarchies, 38
Mark-data pair, 35
Markedness scales, 47

Operation (for parsing), 117–118
Operations Set, 117–120
Optimality. *See* Optimality Theory;
  Optimization